Contents

The Wisdom of the Seasons

The Wisdom of the Seasons

How the Church Year Helps Us
Understand Our Congregational Stories

CHARLES M. OLSEN

THE
ALBAN
INSTITUTE
Herndon, Virginia
www.alban.org

The Alban Institute
2121 Cooperative Way, Suite 100
Herndon, VA 20171

Scripture quotations, unless otherwise noted, are from the New Revised Standard Version of the Bible, copyright © 1989, Division of Christian Education of the National Council of Churches of Christ in the United States of America, and are used by permission.

Chapter 5, pages 111–118, reprinted from *Ending with Hope: A Resource for Closing Congregations*, pages 5–6, by Beth Ann Gaede, ed., with permission from the Alban Institute. Copyright © 2002 by The Alban Institute, Inc. Herndon, VA. All rights reserved.

Chapter 7, pages 156–157, reprinted from John Polkinghorne, *Quantum Physics and Theology: An Unexpected Kinship*, pages 99–104, with permission from Yale University Press. Copyright © 2007 Yale University Press.

Cover design by Tobias Becker, Birdbox Design.

Library of Congress Cataloging-in-Publication Data

Olsen, Charles M.
  The wisdom of the seasons : how the church year helps us understand our congregational stories / Charles M. Olsen.
    p. cm.
  Includes bibliographical references (p. 195).
  ISBN 978-1-56699-396-8
  1. Parishes. 2. Church year. 3. Narrative theology. 4. Church management. I. Title.
  BV700.O67 2009
  269--dc22
                          2009026382

  09   10   11   12   13   VP   5   4   3   2   1

Foreword

Chuck Olsen is ancient.

Please don't misunderstand me. I'm not saying that Chuck Olsen is old, although he is older than me. What I mean is that Chuck Olsen is deeply connected to the ancient wisdom of the Christian tradition, a connection that far too many modern Christians seem to have divorced themselves from in their attempts to stay rooted either in "what we've always done" or in a zeal to create something "new." This makes him an ancient Christian—something like an old soul.

One of the malaises of modern Christianity is that we've lost touch with so much of the ancient traditions of Christianity that were the font of wisdom. I can speculate on why that's so, but I'm not sure I completely understand it other than to say that there seem to be two strains of Christian thought. One is to hold onto the past as tightly as possible until it's no longer possible. The people who adhere to this approach don't hold onto the ancient past. They hold onto the relatively recent past, such as clinging to rituals and routines of the church that were there in their childhood. As a result, many of our churches conduct themselves as though it is still 1965. The other strain of Christian thought is to create a "new" kind of Christianity, one that proclaims itself to be ready for the new wine of Christ that is certain to be poured into their new wineskins. So they are always on the lookout for some new ritual, song, technology, or form of worship.

Chuck Olsen has a heart for something far deeper than our childhood past or our potential future. Chuck understands that real wisdom, the kind of wisdom that connects us with God at the deepest levels, is found when we connect our stories with ancient perceptions and practices that, sadly, are often jettisoned by both groups.

Long ago I realized that while those of ancient times—our Jewish and Christian forebearers—may have lacked the kind of intellectual and technical sophistication we have today, they were abundant with a kind of spiritual wisdom that we now lack. Why else would we still pour over scriptures written 2,000 to 3,500 years ago, searching for wisdom for today? The problem is that while we seek the wisdom of ancient scripture, we don't always seek the wisdom of ancient practices. This seeking of wisdom is where Chuck is gifted. He doesn't always follow the trends, and the result is that he has formed a deep appreciation for ancient wisdom and practices. In previous books, he has been instrumental in guiding the church back to a more prayerful, more Spirit-filled way of being church that has transformed thousands of churches. He did so by recovering the original church's practice of prayer and discernment among pastors, elders, deacons, and leaders.

In his new book, *The Wisdom of the Seasons*, Chuck delves into the wisdom that comes from intentionally and devotionally attending to the Christian seasons as they help us explore our individual and congregational stories, recognizing that the rhythms of the passage of time are a deeply important aspect of Christian spiritual growth.

We modern folk are in such a hurry that we too often have lost contact with how slowing down and attending to the present moment, the holy now, can connect us with God. Hurry kills the spirit because it drains us of patience, humility, openness, and awareness. The more hurried we are, the more self-focused we become. The more we rush, the more we are crushed by the demands of life, leaving us closed off to God and unaware of God's presence in our midst. Chuck Olsen wants us to root our narratives in a pace of worship and a pace of life that opens us more deeply to God's presence. He wants us to recover the natural rhythm of life that Jesus taught us to cultivate.

So much of what Jesus taught used the rhythms of life, experienced by those living in an agricultural society, as the model of growing to spiritual maturity. His metaphors were of sheep and shepherds, seeds and growth, plowing and harvesting, trees and fruit, the passage of the seasons, and knowing what season we are in in our lives. He recognized that there was a wisdom gleaned from the natural world, a wisdom expressed so eloquently by the writer of Ecclesiastes:

> For everything there is a season, and a time for every matter under heaven:
> a time to be born, and a time to die;
> a time to plant, and a time to pluck up what is planted;
> a time to kill, and a time to heal;
> a time to break down, and a time to build up;
> a time to weep, and a time to laugh;
> a time to mourn, and a time to dance;
> a time to throw away stones, and a time to gather stones together…
> —ECCLESIASTES 3:1–5

Jesus understood that life has a rhythm, a cycle of seasons. The cycle is one of newness, growth, harvesting, and death, which becomes preparation for renewal, growth, harvesting, and death, and so on, year after year. This is a cycle that too many modern Christians have lost sight of in their desire to hold onto what is past and comfortable, or in their fervor to create something new and stimulating.

In this book, Chuck begins by asking us to gain a renewed appreciation for spiritual cyclic rhythms that can occur in a day as we intentionally embrace God in the morning, seek God's presence at work, let go of work to be with God in the evening, and then rest in God's embrace at night. This doesn't mean becoming detached from life. It means allowing God's grace and presence to permeate the cycle of our days and the narratives we create to capture, understand, and share our experience, both as individuals and as congregations. He also explores the rhythms of worship, and how each worship service has its own cycle of life.

Chuck's main desire, though, is to help us recapture the wisdom that emerges from paying attention to the liturgical seasons—and they do have a deep wisdom—and that helps us explore our congregation. So many contemporary churches have left behind as archaic and anachronistic the liturgical rhythms of the church year. They may celebrate Christmas, Easter, and Pentecost, but they've lost the connection with the Holy that comes from immersing ourselves in the practices of the seasons of Advent, Lent, and Ordinary Time. Too often, modern Christians want celebration without preparation.

I've discovered this not only in my own church but in many of the newer, nondenominational, "sophisticated" churches. In our own church some people trickle in to worship on Good Friday, but they pour out for Easter. As one member, years ago, said to me about Lent and Good Friday, "It's all so depressing. I want joy. I don't want to think about depressing things like discipline and death." My response to her and others has always been, "How can you truly appreciate the joy if you don't appreciate the sadness?" The discipline of Lent and the sadness of Good Friday prepare people for the joy of Easter. The resurrection of Easter makes no sense without the crucifixion. Without Lent and Good Friday, Easter becomes what it sort of has become: a time to wear nice clothes and eat chocolate. Interestingly enough, a large, nondenominational church near us, recognizing that people want celebration without sadness, has gotten rid of Good Friday completely. They've replaced it with a 66,000-egg Easter-egg hunt on Good Friday in which each child gets a free bag of candy, making that Friday truly "candy-good" rather than transformational good. Another large nondenominational church starts offering

Easter services on Maundy Thursday, allowing people to sleep in on Easter Sunday—all the better to prepare for the chocolate feast to come.

When I was in graduate school, I discovered that African Christians also struggle to appreciate the balancing of Good Friday and Easter, but in a different way. One African Roman Catholic priest from Kenya told me that the people of his country pour out to church on Good Friday, but only dribble in on Easter. His interpretation? That the people of his country know suffering but don't experience much celebration, so they identify with Christ on the cross but not with the risen Christ. They sought community in sadness, and were skeptical of celebration. They struggled to balance sadness and celebration.

I also experience the struggle to get modern Christians to immerse themselves in the liturgical seasons during the season of Advent. What do you think the biggest complaints are among Christians around Christmas? I hear two of them. First, it is that everyone is so busy and so partied out that by the time Christmas rolls around they are exhausted. Second, they complain that people have forgotten that Jesus is the reason for the season. My answer to both is that what afflicts them is their loss of Advent.

Much like Lent, Advent is a season of preparation. It is meant to be a season of prayer and reflection preparing people for the celebrations of Christmas. But we've forgotten that fact because we only like celebration. To the people worn out by Christmas I suggest that they immerse themselves in Advent instead, making it a time of prayer reflection. I tell them, "Go to your parties, but also spend time in quiet and stillness. Let Advent balance Christmas. Let the Christmas season begin on the day that the Christmas season actually begins—Christmas Day." Ironically, we've killed Advent and its potential to uncover wisdom for our own stories, turning it into the Christmas season, and then when the Christmas season rolls around with its twelve days, we put it aside as we rush to celebrate the new year.

To those who complain that we've forgotten that Jesus is the reason for the season, I reply with a rather snobby comment: "And you've forgotten that we are still in Advent, not Christmas. Christmas doesn't start until Christmas day." I was actually taken by surprise one time when an evangelical Christian, one who should have known better, replied, "You're wrong! We're in Christmas! Uh, ... what's Advent?"

The point of my whole digression is that Chuck Olsen reminds us that there is a rhythm to the liturgical year, and if we pay attention to it and participate in it, this rhythm will keep us balanced. The fruit of that balance is that it will open us up more deeply both to God's presence and wisdom. The Wisdom of the Seasons wonderfully reconnects us with ancient traditions that overcome the pace and haste of modern life. We all are moving far too fast, and the result is that we are becoming spiritually poorer. Our spirits are being crushed by the pace of modern life, and it doesn't help when our churches match that pace by forgetting to invite people into an alternative life—one lived at a pace that Jesus practiced.

I wish you all the blessings in the world as you—bringing with you your personal church stories—embark on a journey through the rhythms of the season with Chuck Olsen, as this very wise and ancient man (ancient in the sense of his connection with the life Jesus and his followers lived) guides us to recapture the wisdom that comes with living intentionally in the seasons of the Christian year.

Blessings on you.

N. Graham Standish
Pastor, Calvin Presbyterian Church, Zelienople, Pennsylvania, and author of *Becoming a Blessed Church* and *Humble Leadership*

Preface

About ten years ago, the invitation to conduct a leadership training event for church board members on Long Island, New York, carried an interesting additional request. Tom Castlen, the presbytery executive, invited me to take a block of time to try out something new—something that I had been thinking about but had not published. I readily took him up on his generous offer. In this training event for leadership teams from congregations, I had introduced the important place of history and storytelling at the church board level and the corresponding practice of reflecting biblically and theologically on those stories. By weaving congregational narratives with sources from the biblical tradition—people, events, places, teachings—I led them to glean values, deeply held beliefs, and to a recognition of God's presence in their own experiences. Over the years our organization, Worshipful-Work, had learned that many attempts to reflect biblically and theologically bog down because folks do not think they know enough about the Bible to engage in this practice. So now a new opportunity arose. What if this group of board members entered Scripture through the passageway of the seasons of the church year? What if the three major festivals that celebrate God's presence became a motif through which church leadership groups could look at their own stories? What might a trinitarian spirituality look like through this model? What wisdom might be mined from the seasons of the church year to help us understand our congregational stories?

So, during the experimental phase of this conference, I engaged the participants in a series of exercises to match their own congregational stories with specific seasons of the church year. (See chapter 7 for details.) The participants responded with a great deal of interest and enthusiasm. The possibility of writing a new book emerged from that experiment, and I knew that sooner or later the book would need to be written. I laid it aside for the time being, resisting the time and effort that a new book would take. I was already working on several other writing projects, but did write it in summary form for a chapter, "Trinitarian Spirituality and Decision Making: A Structure for Congregational Stories," which I contributed to *The Hidden Spirit: Discovering the Spirituality of Institutions*.[1] (This book expands on that chapter.)

Over the ensuing years, as I read timely articles and shared informal conversations with friends, I was continually reminded of that earlier experiment and the seeds that had been planted there. When I heard church stories, I increasingly pictured them through the lens of the church seasons. They just seemed to fit together. And I began to connect my own life experiences to the seasons of the church year as well.

In the past, when a book was completed, I uttered a sigh of relief, saying, "Thank God that is finished. Never again!" Even though I continued to include information and training designs about stories and the seasons of the church year in training sessions I led, I resisted doing another book. Problematic health issues that spanned several years gave me an additional excuse. And my wife did not encourage me to write another book. She said writing a book is like being pregnant—totally consuming of time and energy. I did occasionally think about the book, but I also wondered if anyone would be interested in the subject. Even if others might find a book useful, I questioned whether I was the person to write it and found other excuses for letting the idea slide. I became involved in local community issues. My wife and I love to travel and engage in outdoor recreational activities. Retirement from professional ministry was supposed to offer time for that! But in spite of my resistance, the nudge to write this book never went away.

Then one year ago, in 2008, I attended a Five Day Academy for Spiritual Formation sponsored by Upper Room Ministries. I decided to go without any agenda or expectations other than to worship. In the first evening's listening circle, I coyly introduced myself without reference to professional status or my life work. The next morning the lecturer, Stephanie Ford, a professor of Christian Spirituality at Earlham School of Religion, Richmond, Indiana, "outed" me by referring to some of my former work and writings to the assembled group. She then introduced a salient theme—that each of us has a vocation, regardless of one's job or active professional status or even retirement. She seemed to look straight at me!

In the hour of silent reflective time that followed, my own sense of vocation to serve the ecumenical church came back. I remembered that, early in my ministry, John Miller, a Mennonite from Kitchener, Ontario, told me I needed to think of myself as an apostle. When asked what that meant, he said, "An apostle is one who encourages others by traveling around the church listening to and telling stories." As I looked back on my ministry in lay renewal initiatives, Project Base Church, and Worshipful-Work, it had been exactly that. I was always most energized by interaction with a wide variety of denominations and identified the ecumenical world as my locus for ministry. That was my vocation.

That same evening of the academy, I returned to my little listening circle with a larger story. I could not hide my full story and came clean with them. By the next evening they had assumed the role of a clearness committee out of the Quaker tradition, and the issue of whether or not to write this book became a major question for spiritual discernment. I named for them what I would need to let go of in order to move ahead—the fears and blockages that had prevented me. By the last evening, I took hold of a calling and declared my intention to write. Their blessing and encouragement attested to the inner call of God, whose presence I experienced in their midst as the loving body of Christ.

Confirmation of the discernment came with an invitation from the Alban Institute to consider writing this book. Having had a close association with Alban over the years in personal relationships, training, and publishing, contributing this book offered an additional opportunity to share their vision and ministry for narrative leadership. Loren Mead, the founder, had encouraged me to write the learnings from a project on small group development from Project Base Church in the early 1980s. Jim Wind, the current president, became a mentor as I designed a model for church board development in the early 1990s when he was a program director for Lilly Endowment. That model, presented in an earlier Alban publication, *Transforming Church Boards into Communities of Spiritual Leaders,* led to the founding of Worshipful-Work.

Last fall on a personal retreat at the Trappist monastery in Snowmass, Colorado, I took the invitation to write a book proposal with me. In the beauty and stillness of that setting, the outline and shape for this book unfolded. When the decision to write was made, I sensed God's leading and felt energized and willing to commit the effort it would take.

The consolation, as the Jesuits would say, for this discernment process came when Alban assigned Beth Ann Gaede to an editing role. I had worked with her on a previous project and have come to appreciate again her wisdom in shaping the manuscript and her personal grace as a working colleague.

With the work of this book, I have done much letting go. I have experienced God's unusual presence. And now I take hold to offer it as a gift to the church I love.

The Eternal Rhythm of Spiritual Formation

Over the past several years, I have had the opportunity to work with leadership groups from a wide variety of congregations, primarily church boards and councils in retreat and seminar settings. During those sessions, we looked at their stories, both individual and communal. I gained several quick impressions. Some groups attempt to tell who they are as a congregation by offering static definitions: "We are . . ." or "We think . . ." But others disclose who they are by relating what they do—how they acted during a series of events and what they learned from those experiences. When listening to the latter, I pictured them on a journey, having seen where they have been, how they moved, and where they are heading. Some church boards grasped that their church story was part of an extended journey. Others did not. Little gray area could be found between the two.

Then a watershed awareness surfaced for me. The boards either recognized that God had a role in their story or God was out of mind, out of sight. When asked about the absence of any reference to God's role in their story, board members often said, "Well, we assumed that!" But God's presence had not been acknowledged.

Then I made another observation: Congregations that have a sense of story or journey and the awareness that God plays a role in their story tend to be congregations of vital faith. They can move forward with energy and vision. New people who visit them immediately pick up on their energy and are attracted to that church. The church's lived experience, projected through their stories and subsequent reflections, becomes a powerful witness to visitors. Conversely, congregations that have no sense of story or journey—and little awareness of God playing a role in their stories—tend to be congregations of lethargic faith. They tend to get stuck in the past. New people who visit them pick that up as well and are not attracted to such communities.

The importance of storytelling to the life of a congregation is certainly not new. Christian educators have relied upon it in their classrooms for years. Stories are a valuable communication tool in preaching. Life stories readily find their way into pastoral counseling sessions and spiritual direction journals. Writers of congregational histories look for a wide range of clues with which to construct a "thick history," which Jim Wind of the Alban Institute advocates and which points to the quality of life, style, or character of the congregation.

Church leaders, while they search for new programs or strategic plans for the future, often overlook and ignore the rich treasure that is close at hand. But in the active practice of story formation and reflection, a jewel emerges that can help the church deepen and extend its spiritual life. Leadership teams have an opportunity to claim a gift that lies figuratively right beneath their own journeying feet!

Since the awareness and recital of communal stories, accompanied by a sense of journey and an awareness of God's role in the story, are important keys to developing congregational life, how can stories be nurtured? Church leaders can begin forming corporate memory by telling their own stories about concrete congregational experiences. Then the leaders can connect the congregation's experiences with aspects of the biblical tradition and discover what values and meanings are vitally important for their common and future life together. They will more easily generate new meanings, insights, and visions if they are already familiar with motifs or structures through which they can examine their own stories. What might those structures be?

The late James F. Hopewell, a professor at Candler School of Theology in Atlanta, looked to classic story lines in his search to find each congregation's distinctive story and identity.[1] He looked at congregations' settings, stories, symbols, values, and patterns. He looked for clues to a "plot" and followed the ways that it thickened, unfolded, and twisted. In addition, he looked for attitudes toward the world and the future so that he might discover a congregation's fundamental vision. He drew upon four basic literary categories to type the congregations—*comic, romantic, tragic,* and *ironic.* Each type of congregation tended to look at the world and to its future from a particular posture. Hopewell's monumental work suggests that congregations might understand and maximize their stories through particular frameworks.

I believe the seasons of the church year, a long and deep faith tradition that lies close at hand, offer a potential framework for congregational stories. Yes, the story of the life of Christ is told through Christmas and Easter celebrations. But the seasons also tell the story of the church. Could the wisdom inherent in this tradition possibly offer a structure for our own communal stories? I believe it can. The seasons of the grand story easily connect and interweave with our stories. This book will not offer a study of the church seasons per se. But it will offer a way to understand our congregation's stories by examining them through the wisdom of the church seasons. Active story weaving between congregational stories and the great stories in the biblical tradition that are imbedded in the church seasons carries the potential to form and deepen our faith, transform congregations, and reframe old stories for a new day. I have discovered that stories are really jewels of great value, not to be ignored, passed over, or discounted. When they are valued and processed within the structure of a familiar and trusted tradition, they hold the key to transforming the church's life and ministry.

The common themes that thread through the seasons of the church year can be found in the discipline of spiritual direction—most often seen in a relationship between a spiritual director and the directee. (Some denominations are more familiar with group direction with the director occupying the pulpit.) The director's gifts and energies focus upon the stories of the directee. An attentive director listens for three primary movements in spiritual formation: *letting go, naming God's presence,* and *taking hold.*

LETTING GO

As a spiritual director listens, she or he will ask, How and where is this person letting go? What is being relinquished and laid aside? Where is she or he surrendering to the love and grace of God? Are any experiences being withheld from God out of fear that letting go of them will reduce a person to a mere nothing? We are constantly faced with the need to say goodbye to valued relationships, unmet dreams, careers, health, or youth. And we are called to say goodbye to habits and practices that poison relationships, health, and a productive life. Most critically, we are invited to let go of ego—driven self-centeredness—thereby allowing God to direct and run our agendas.

But we fear letting go in favor of holding on to what Thomas Merton calls our "false self." We attempt to define ourselves with familiar and important categories from the surrounding culture, so we hold on, lest we be reduced to being nobodies. The dying unto self that Jesus commends confronts us as individuals and makes us uncomfortable. Corporate bodies face the same call and resulting discomfort. I ask congregations these questions: As you look at your own story, where have you had to let go—only to discover that you let God? Or, What are you willing to allow to die in you in order to receive the gifts and growth that God can offer? The questions are often followed by stunned silence. We don't like to think that way. But we need help to begin to do so.

NAMING GOD'S PRESENCE

I agreed to offer oversight to a DMin candidate who was in a spiritual direction program. We looked together at the verbatims he had produced of the sessions in which he provided direction. I was impressed with the number of times he asked directees for impressions or awareness of God's presence. Over the series of weekly sessions the directees became more and more comfortable with the question and more likely to cite experiences in which they were aware of God's presence.

While leading training events for church boards, I would begin a warm-up by putting the participants in triads for a quick round of standing conversations. They were to respond to my promptings from their own experience of board meetings: Relate your experience of saying yes to the invitation to join the board. Relate an experience on the board when you were moved or touched in a significant way—to tears, laughter, insight, and so forth. Relate a moment of surprise in a meeting. In response to these promptings, the room would buzz with animated conversations. Then came a zinger: Relate an awareness that you and your board had of God's presence. Typically an awkward silence would follow until a few voices broke the silence. Lay leadership groups do not tend to think or talk with one another about signs of God's presence in their work. They defer to the religious professionals for that.

Naming God's presence within the framework of the seasons of the church year opens a path that is both old and new. When individual spiritual directees or church leadership groups become more comfortable with the practice of naming God's presence, they will notice recurring patterns. They will name God's presence three ways—a trinitarian framework. At times they will note that God is a loving and wise provider whose ways seem beyond their capacity to fully comprehend. At times they will describe God as close and caring, entering into a graceful and understanding relationship with them. At other times they will sense that God lies deeply within their hearts, encouraging and comforting them along the journey of faith.

Vasileios of Stavronikita, a monk from Mount Athos, a region in northern Greece known as a center of Eastern Orthodox monasticism, said, "Whoever has really seen the church has seen the Holy Trinity." In other words, if we listen to the stories of the church long enough, we will hear the different ways in which God has been experienced. In the early Christian church, a trinitarian affirmation of faith was not simply constructed from a rational process but was rooted in the community's experiences of God. This awareness became a central organizing structure for the creeds of the early church and offered a way to teach new adherents about faith in a living God. The church knew this one God as a loving, giving, creating God who entered into relationship with people. *God existed beyond them*—all-powerful, all-knowing, exercising both faithful love and judgment. They also affirmed that God was present to them in the person of *Jesus*—*God with us* who knows our suffering and humanity. And they experienced God's presence in the *Holy Spirit*—*God in us* comforting, enlightening, reminding, pointing, empowering, and innerving.

As we name God's presence within our own stories and connect them to the festivals of the church seasons—Christmas, Easter, and Pentecost—we will see God's threefold presence. We can affirm this presence from reflection on our own real-life stories. Trinitarian spiritual formation will be rooted not only in philosophical and rational categories but also in tangible experiences within the believing community. Placing our stories within the framework of the Trinity gives us a practical way to talk about them within the faith community and to witness to those who inquire about the faith that lies within us. Relating life experience to the Trinity has always been a time-honored way to make sense out of and find meaning in our stories in the light of the grand story of God's creation, redemption, and sanctification in the world.

Several years ago in my opening address to the national Ecumenical Interim Ministry Network, I introduced the rhythm of spiritual formation within the structure of the church year. Marva Dawn, a prolific author on Christian spiritual formation, was in attendance and later wrote, "After his keynote address in which he listed several examples, I found myself filling out the entire calendar of Christian seasons and was delighted to see how helpful his notion is for understanding the complete church year."[2]

TAKING HOLD

Finally, the spiritual director looks to the directee's story to discern ways this person is taking hold—aligning with and investing in what God cares about in order to make a difference. Taking hold springs from a deep sense of vocation—ministering in God's name in the world. Old boundaries are stretched and broken. New visions for the world of God's reign take shape.

Working with a congregation's long history and recent narratives should not imprison church leaders in a past but free and energize them to reframe their stories for a new future into which they can move. The power of the major festivals of Christmas, Easter, and Pentecost—each containing a triad of anticipation, celebration, and proclamation—propels the church to proclaim and send forth.

The one, two, three rhythm of letting go, naming God's presence, and taking hold is basic to spiritual direction and is also present in multiple Christian practices. In the first chapters of this book, we will examine that rhythm in the various practices and consider it in the time frames of moments, hours, days, weeks, and finally in the seasons of the church year.

CHAPTER I

The Eternal Rhythm
in Spiritual Practice

As you move through this book, you are headed toward engaging your church stories with the seasons of the church year, in which you will sense the resonance between the two. You will also discover that the eternal rhythm of letting go, naming God's presence, and taking hold beats within them. But before you arrive in that holy space, we would do well to visit other expressions of the threefold rhythm along the way.

This chapter identifies a variety of spiritual practices. Each one may be envisioned as a stepping-stone in a garden. As you review them, I invite you to take a brief step on each to consider them all or to tarry on a limited number for closer examination. These stepping-stones originate from the rich tradition of spiritual practice. Some are familiar. Others may seem strange. Some are well worn through constant use. Others may appear to be fresh, new, or unused. Some offer comfort. Others appear to look slippery and threatening. As we visit the stepping-stones of spiritual practice, you may dance through them, selecting those that appear most inviting. Or you may proceed deliberately, as though marching in a parade. Whatever method you consider, the rhythmic one, two, three in the movement of spiritual formation will engrain itself in your spiritual psyche. The practices that follow are not presented in any particular order.

BREATHING

As the ancient church developed an interest in practices of prayer that would deepen members' faith in Christ, many became curious about Paul's admonition to "pray without ceasing" (1 Thess. 5:17). How could this be done? A tradition that developed in the sixth-century Eastern Church came to be known as "the Jesus Prayer" and is practiced to this day. The prayer is attached to the rhythms of breathing so that both inhaling and exhaling carry the prayer. In its longer version, the in breath carries, "Lord Jesus Christ, Son of Abraham," and the out breath carries, "Have mercy upon me a sinner." A shorter version articulates, "Lord Jesus Christ . . . have mercy on me" with each rise and fall of the breath. A still shorter prayer speaks, "Lord . . . have mercy." This ancient prayer is repeated in what we have come to know in the liturgy as the Kyrie, "Lord, have mercy on me. Christ, have mercy on me. Lord, have mercy on me." The Kyrie is one of the oldest prayers in Christian tradition, recorded in Jesus's story of the tax collector who went up to the temple to pray. He did not pray like the Pharisee who said, "God, I thank you that I am not like other people." But he prayed, "God, be merciful to me, a sinner!" (Luke 18:11, 13).

In the Jesus Prayer, the longer or shorter version may be connected to the rise and fall of breathing and then repeated over and over again. Those who engage in this form of prayer attest to its transforming power. Initially, the breath carries the prayer. But after a time, the prayer carries the breath. Then the person may go about her or his work and regular activities while being in constant prayer—a prayer offered via the eternal rhythm without even thinking the words. In the initial phase of the Jesus Prayer, letting go, a form of self-relinquishment, occurs. At the moment of transformation, one is aware of God's presence, and while engaging in the work of the day, one takes hold.

Across the years, various traditions have learned their own particular style of praying with the rhythm of breathing. One pattern in the African American church illustrates this. A practitioner instructed me to first go to a quiet, secluded place, then concentrate on the rising and falling of my breath. She instructed, "As your lungs fill with air, pause and think of something or someone that is stealing your energy. Then on the out breath, lay that aside by flushing it out and move to the next . . . and so on. After a while you will have laid aside all concerns to which you are giving energy. That is a moment of stillness. Don't think. Just be in God's presence. You may conclude the stillness by praying the Lord's Prayer—even attaching that prayer to the rising and falling of your breath. Finally, with each new breath, allow concerns of the day to come back to you one by one. On the in breath, allow a concern to enter. On the out breath, ask yourself if there is anything you can do about it today. If there is, decide what to do. If not, give it to God and wrap it in the mercy of God."

Notice here again the rhythm—letting go, naming God's presence, and taking hold. Various forms of breath prayer all incorporate them. They combine functions of the physical body with mental concentration and spiritual energy into a wholeness of being.

CENTERING PRAYER

Centering prayer offers a way to listen to God beyond words, thoughts, images, or perceptions. The silent method facilitates going into the center of one's being in order to be aware of the presence of God within. Some refer to it as the "Prayer of the Cloud," drawing from the fourteenth-century classic *The Cloud of Unknowing*. In recent years, centering prayer has been popularized by Father Thomas Keating at a Trappist monastery near Snowmass, Colorado. The method is often practiced in an extended silent retreat. Centering prayer is not a technique designed to produce an anticipated outcome or simply to clear the mind. The person who prays consents to be in relationship with God. When thoughts come, they are to be gently dismissed with use of a chosen sacred word in order to refocus on being in the presence of God.

A centering prayer practitioner, Carol Powell, describes her experience of a Ten Day Post Intensive Centering Prayer Retreat:

> Why do I do it? When I sit with the Lord in the silence of those ten days I bring with me all aspects of my life, my joys, my problems, my frustrations, my virtues, my faults, my efforts and my failures. I come just as I am with nothing hidden. . . . It is not always easy to be quiet with God. Illusions are shattered. Reality has a way of intruding itself when there are no distractions and one is in complete silence. Each time, though, in some way I am eventually graced with a version of the whole and what my place is in the total scheme of things. In some way I experience connectedness to God, everyone else and to the whole universe. And there is an inner unity within myself. . . . Silence purifies thoughts and words. It tames the ego and enables one to listen to the Lord, to oneself, and only then, is it possible to listen to other people.[1]

The eternal rhythms are obvious in Carol's testimony. Letting go of words, thoughts, images, or perceptions does not come easily. Taking hold by aligning with the divine purpose comes purely out of the grace of God's presence. Even when the person who prays surfaces his or her own pain, or recalls the deep pain of others in the world, the pain will not be resisted but is to be offered to God. All three movements are present in the quietness of centering prayer.

DIRECTIONAL POSITIONING

The late Joseph Smerke, a Crosier father who resided at his order's monastery in Hastings, Nebraska, was an unusual spiritual director. He liked to draw upon different traditions in his spiritual walk, so he prepared one room in the retreat house with Native American symbols and artifacts. He also drew a practice of prayer from the Native American medicine wheel, a ritual that began by facing the rising sun with hands raised in prayer. He prayed in this special room with raised hands in four directional positions. Facing east with the rising sun, he prayed to draw spiritual energy, to take hold of the tasks of the day. Facing west toward the setting sun, he engaged in self-examination and confession in order to let go. Facing north, he sought wisdom. And facing south, he allowed for happy thoughts. North and south positions affirmed God's presence that came to him in wisdom and understanding. Religious practices from other cultures offer great gifts of understanding basic faith and trust. Blessed are those who access them and then have the ability to translate them for our use!

LECTIO DIVINA

The *lectio divina*, divine reading, offers a time-honored practice of coming to Scripture in a prayerful way. It has been embraced and expressed through the rules of saints like Augustine, Benedict, and Basil. Its origins can be traced to the Middle Ages. A twelfth-century book offered four steps for a "Monk's Ladder," that is, reading, reflecting, praying, and contemplating God's presence in the text. An increasing number of individuals and groups are resurrecting the practice for the church today. On September, 16, 2005, in the courtyard of the papal summer residence of Castel Gandolfo, Pope Benedict XVI commended the practice of the *lectio divina* to four hundred adherents during the International Congress on "Sacred Scripture in the Life of the Church." He presented it as "a diligent reading of Sacred Scripture accompanied by prayer [that] brings about that intimate dialogue in which the person reading Scripture hears God who is speaking, and in praying, responds to him with trusting openness of heart."[2]

The method begins with a time of letting go in relaxation, clearing the mind of thoughts and concerns. Deep breathing—perhaps attaching and repeating a word or phrase—frees the participant for the engagement. The lectio then moves through four stages, beginning with a slow and repeated reading of a selected scripture. First, one tastes the text, then mulls it over. Chewing applies it to one's own life. Then the text is savored, and God's sweet presence invites conversation. Finally, in digesting the text, the reader becomes aligned with the cares of God. Participants, tangibly influenced by the total experience, take hold in a new and different way. Although designed for use by individuals, the method can help a group read Scripture devotionally, in contrast to a rational, analytic approach. It allows for the imagination to roam within silent spaces.

WALKING THE LABYRINTH

In 1220 workers laid a forty-foot-wide labyrinth of blue and white stone in the floor of the Chartres Cathedral in France. In recent years the practice of walking a labyrinth has been rediscovered and now finds a home in many churches and retreat centers. The labyrinth is not simply a maze that offers many routes to reach a single destination—some of them deceptive—but rather contains only one path to the center, a path that then returns to the starting place. Prior to entering, the walker thinks about the concerns and questions that he or she would like to take on the walk. Letting go may be symbolized by removal of shoes. The path, with its many twists and turns, offers a mirror or reminder of the twists and turns in one's own life journey. The walker allows decisions that were made and not made to come to mind. Both life's burdens and delights accompany the pilgrim as joys and sorrows surface and are released. On the way into the center, one's heart and mind are gradually opened to the anticipated still point at the center. This first stage is called purgation—a releasing and letting go of the agendas of life, the stresses we carry, and the distractions that blind us. One may move to the center quickly or take an extended time to relinquish the burdens of life. Other people may be walking at the same time, but each keeps to his or her own path and tends to ignore the others.

As the walker reaches the center, a small round space—the second stage, *illumination*—surfaces. This is holy ground, a place for clarity, wisdom, and insight. One may sit in silence, kneel, read, or even hum a tune. The walker may ask, "What unearned gift am I open to receive here?" It is gracious space. A gift may be claimed before beginning to move out. Even if a tangible gift does not come, awareness of God's presence may be the sufficient gift. Many like to tarry in the center, as though resting in the womb or hand of God.

The outward returning movement brings the third stage, union, in which the pilgrim brings a new vision or spirit back to daily life. One is empowered to do the work to which one has been called. Taking hold may express itself in thanks for the gifts that have been received, along with a commitment to use them in one's calling and ministry. The labyrinth offers a concrete experience of the threefold eternal rhythm of spiritual formation.

WALKING OR JOGGING

Walking or running for three miles may not seem like a religious practice to some, but others of us can attest to the inner movements of the Spirit while striding the path. Many people have told me about becoming stuck in their work, especially when the work is mentally taxing. Then they decided to go for a walk for at least fifteen minutes. They returned refreshed. Ideas once again flowed. What happens? The time away in physical activity reflects more than a change of pace. The movement of letting go accompanies the walker while he or she pays attention to the surrounding environment. Without expecting any predetermined result of the walk, the walker is free to discover and receive whatever may present itself on the journey.

I have been a jogger for forty years, and I find that in addition to offering a way to let go of the tensions of daily life, jogging offers an opportunity to practice meditation on God's presence and love. I like to begin at a slow pace while releasing. Then as my breathing increases in tempo and intensity, I connect the pace of breathing to the pace of my steps—at first one breath per three strides, and then one per two strides. I add scripture phrases to the rising and falling of my breath and repeat them over and over with two steps for each part of the phrase, such as "Bless the Lord . . . O my soul," "Praise God . . . from whom blessings flow," "The Lord's my shepherd . . . I shall not want," "Nothing . . . separates us from God's love," or "The heavens declare . . . the glory of God." The psalms and familiar hymns offer rich meditative material. Body, mind, and soul harmonize together in awareness of God's presence. Finally, every jogger knows that a slowed down walk for cooling off fosters a healthy conclusion to the workout. I use this walk to determine what is important to take hold of in the next leg of my life's journey.

EATING TOGETHER

Christian liturgies of worship have roots not only in the temple but also at the table. House church gatherings for the early Christian community were table fellowships for sharing letters of the apostles, food, prayers, and mutual support. The apostle Paul chides some participants for behaving in selfish ways, including hoarding food and drink. He commends humility and hospitality as a rule of conduct. When at table, one's own needs and appetites are to be subject to concern and love for the sister and brother. One simply cannot eat at a fellowship table without letting go of the urge to stuff one's stomach with food while the neighbor remains hungry. Bringing food, sharing food, giving God thanks for food, and taking food to the needy incorporate the threefold eternal rhythm of spiritual formation.

Moreover, at that same table the bread of Christ's presence is broken and the cup of his love is poured out with thanksgiving to God for all of God's mercies. The powerful manifestation of this rhythm drives deep into the human spirit. Christ, who took the form of a servant and yielded his own life for a hostile world out of love for God, took hold of God's call. He embodied the eternal rhythms.

Some faith communities, such as the Church of the Brethren, maintain a grand and powerful tradition of feet washing while at the love feast table. Following the example of Jesus in the upper room with his disciples on that fateful eve of his death, they stoop to their knees in humility to wash one another's feet. Jesus challenged the pride of his disciples when he stooped to wash their feet, even as he heard them arguing about who was greatest. Even so, those who engage in this powerful practice have to first let go of a huge amount of pride and self-oriented dignity.

FASTING

Jesus assumes that his followers will engage in the practice of fasting. He began his own ministry by entering into a forty-day fast, after the pattern of Moses's years in the wilderness. Fasting offers a practical path to clarity and understanding about one's own identity and calling—a way of discernment. As he wrestled with his own temptations, Jesus concluded that he would choose humility over power, poverty over wealth, and trust in God over popularity.

The letting go in fasting is obvious—the denial of food for a season. John Wesley's personal practice reflected the custom of the Anglican Church during Lent. He affirmed that the fast fixes our eyes firmly on God for God's own glory, acknowledging that the Word of God alone suffices for all needs. His own practice began on Thursday evening—reminding him of the events of the Last Supper—and lasted until midafternoon Friday, reminding him of the death of Christ. (Some note with a twist of humor that the end of his fast also coincided with British teatime!)

Marjorie Thompson, staff member for programs of spiritual formation with Upper Room, points out that "fasting reveals our excessive attachments and the assumptions that lie behind them. Food is necessary to life, but we have made it more necessary than

God. How often have we neglected to remember God's presence when we would never consider neglecting to eat! Fasting brings us face to face with how we put the material world ahead of its spiritual Source."[3] Letting go of the immediate need for food, and longing for fulfillment in mystical union with God (presence), is a difficult but obvious movement. The movement of taking hold is subtler. For Jesus, fasting was always tied to almsgiving and prayer. He illustrated this in his teachings from the Sermon on the Mount. The early church fathers taught that the money saved by denying food should be shared with widows, orphans, and people in need so that others may benefit from this expression of humility. People of faith also fast in solidarity with and pray for victims of violence, injustice, or poverty; both fasting and intercessory prayer are tangible ways of taking hold.

SACRED DANCE

Liturgical dance has become a meaningful communication form and powerful worship component for many people. King David, who stripped down to a linen ephod and danced at the head of a procession while bringing the Ark of the Covenant from the rural hinterland to the new national capital in Jerusalem, is a case in point. He was genuinely excited to bring the Ark to his home capital. His conduct was an expression of divine worship, for he was dancing "before the LORD with all his might" (2 Sam. 6:14). But his wife Michal, daughter of the court of King Saul, saw a different picture. Her reaction led to a bitter argument when David returned home to bless his family. She accused him of being a vulgar fellow who shamefully uncovered himself in front of all the maidens—an embarrassment to his house and nation. He replied that he was dancing before the Lord and not for the girls—who, by the way, would hold him in honor.

Sacred movement frequently finds its way into religious celebrations. A congregation I served in Grand Island, Nebraska, was graced for the season of Lent in 1985 by three women from the

Sacred Dance Group of Boulder, Colorado. Their gifts and spirit became a vital and enriching part of every worship gathering. But they could not have offered this gift without letting go of inhibitions. They had to release many fears and focus on the message they were trying to communicate. Many worshipers in the congregation were movingly led into the presence of God by a practice without words.

The Shaker sect in eighteenth-century America was noted for its communal dancing. On dance evenings each person would spend a half hour alone in silence, purging fears and purifying thoughts. Then all would gather in the dance hall with men and women forming separate lines. The purpose of the dance was to liberate the soul and invite inhabitation of the Spirit. After a word of wisdom spoken by an elder who was positioned between the two lines, they began to silently move in swaying procession around the room to the accompaniment of several singers. They paused later to form a large oblong circle to see if any dancer had received the gift of any additional expressions of dance. (One witness reported that several girls joined hands and swirled in circles until they were exhausted.) If so, it would be expressed. They let go in order to dance, became open to God's giving presence in the dance, and responded by taking hold of a new form of dance if they were so moved.

After viewing an interpretive dance in a contemporary worship service, one rather hostile man confronted the female dancer with, "Young lady, what did you mean by that?" She responded, "If I could have told you, I would not have had to dance it!" Some practices go beyond words.

KNEELING

Various body positions assist offering prayer, but none is more symbolic than kneeling. In that position one *lets go* of pride, power, and self-importance, making oneself vulnerable to positive or negative actions of others. Humility bends us to position ourselves to receive a gift or blessing. Historically, kneeling (or even falling prostrate) may have been accompanied by dressing in sackcloth and ashes—a symbol of repentance and shame.

As a child, I clearly remember stumbling into my parents' bedroom at bedtime to discover both of them on their knees saying their nightly prayers aloud. That powerful memory has stayed with me across the years of my life. My wife also recalls powerful moments related to kneeling. When visiting her grandparents one weekend per month, she participated in their morning family prayers. She sat on a small footstool at her grandfather's side while he stood tall to read the Bible. Then all of the family dropped to their knees for prayer. She treasures that small stool on which she knelt in Grandpa's house, and the stool now graces our living room. We both trace the spiritual heritage of our families to this humble practice. It is reinforced when I hear the stories of other people having been on their knees in some significant place or time. The message that comes to the kneeler in prayer may be different from the message that comes to a jogger.

A steelworker friend in western Pennsylvania told me his story: "I am a rather plain, ordinary man and have some serious health limitations. Since getting out of bed is difficult for me, I tend to roll out of bed in the morning onto my knees—propping myself up with my elbows on the bed. While I am in this position, I might as well pray. So every morning I pray this prayer: 'God, I love you. What are you up to today? Let me be a part of it!'" His kneeling position of submission and openness triggered letting go. His love for God tipped off his awareness of God's presence. Aligning himself with God's purposes led him to take hold.

LAYING ON HANDS

The sick room in a family residence or the kneeling rail of a chapel are often settings in which those present offer prayers for wholeness of body, mind, and spirit. The elders of the church gather at the invitation of a person in need. Admitting a need, then acknowledging that need before others, and finally subjecting oneself to the ritual of laying on of hands requires much letting go. We prefer to be self-reliant and self-sufficient, to fulfill our own needs. We find it difficult to ask for help. But a request for prayers of healing accompanied with laying on of hands fosters a major turning to God. This ritual embraces mystery, spirit, freedom, and power. There are no guarantees of healing. No particular outcomes can be demanded. The person in need places herself or himself in the presence of a loving God, attended by fellow members of the church. Any subsequent form of wholeness that results will be determined only by God. Taking hold will not necessarily lead to "taking up the bed to walk." It may express itself in patient waiting, hope, and specific practices that aid the healing process.

Setting apart a leader for specific service and ordaining her or him for a designated function within the faith community invites similar postures. Most often the new leader kneels before authorities in the church—bishops, clergy, or elders. Holy vows call for renouncing the old life and committing to a new life subject to the community's beliefs, authority, and mission. Letting go may seem transitory. Sensing God's presence may be fleeting. But taking hold demands a life of dedication and service.

THE *EXAMEN*

Ignatius of Loyola developed a method of self-examination that could lead the believer to grow in virtue and holiness. He called the process "the examination of conscience." The *examen*, a shorthand term identified in his spiritual exercise, was to be utilized twice a day, once in the afternoon and once before retiring at night. This practice has grown and been adapted over the years, expanding Paul's admonition, "Don't let the sun go down on your anger" (Eph. 4:26). It serves as a letting go discipline toward the end of the day. It begins with thanksgiving to an ever-present God for the gifts and graces that have been experienced that day. Then it moves to awareness of the sins of the day—not only awareness of actions but also examination of thoughts—tracing them hour by hour. Finally, the believer asks for forgiveness and makes resolution to amend one's life with the help of God's grace. All three movements in the rhythm of spiritual formation shine forth from the prism of the *examen*.

MAKING RETREAT

For several years in the early 1990s I hosted and led retreats at the Heartland Presbyterian Center near Kansas City. In welcoming arriving retreatants to a conference center, I invited them to identify what they left behind in order to attend. The responses included time demands, relationships, tasks, and difficulties. Their journey to the center had already put them in a frame of mind for letting go. When planners fix a location for a new retreat center, they often place it some distance away from centers of activity rather than at a nearby convenient location. Why? They want to give retreatants an opportunity to disengage while traveling.

The back side of the entrance gate sign to the Center, where many of Worshipful-Work's leadership development events were located, says, "Go serve." People leaving a retreat are reminded to take hold of their call to service. In addition, all of the fireplace mantels at the center contained the same admonition. I wanted to write "Come rest" on the front of each sign and over the entrance doors as well, in order to project a balanced retreat experience. The ethos of most congregations, however, tends to be more action oriented. Church leaders are more interested in planning future ministries than they are in reflecting on their past stories and resting in the presence of God. They tend to resist silence and reflection.

When I lead retreats for individuals, I encourage them to find a quiet place for solitude, either in one of the buildings or while walking on the grounds. I say, "As you move about the grounds or the buildings, find a quiet place and notice what is around you. Allow yourself to be drawn to a particular object or setting. This object is an expression of God's good creation. Take time to look at it, noticing its beauty and form. Give thanks to God for it. Trace the history of its development, how it came to be what it is today. Then when you are ready, allow thoughts and concerns that you are carrying to go out to it and be absorbed in it. Let them go. Take time to sit with the object or in the setting as an exercise in contemplation. After a time of stillness, gradually allow the strength and beauty of this object to come to you. Receive it as a gift from God. Take hold of that gift. Think of ways that gift can enhance your ministry." Retreat centers or favorite places for solitude provide excellent settings for both individuals and groups to experience the rhythm of the three movements in spiritual formation.

GOING ON PILGRIMAGE

The religious pilgrimage expands on the personal retreat in time, distance, and scope. A destination is identified where God's presence will be recognized or symbolized. Jerusalem and its temple were such a destination for pilgrims in ancient Israel. A cluster of psalms (120–134) represents songs that pilgrims sang on their way up to Jerusalem. Its location at three thousand feet above sea level resulted in a difficult uphill climb. The pilgrimage would finally be rewarded with a sudden view of the beautiful city set on a hill and with the grandeur of the temple and grounds. Each of these psalms is titled "A Song of Ascents," drawn from the incline of the terrain. Psalm 122 begins:

> I was glad when they said to me,
> "Let us go to the house of the LORD" . . .
> Jerusalem—built as a city
> that is bound firmly together.
> To it the tribes go up, . . .
> to give thanks to the name of the LORD.

Psalm 121 attests to the difficulty and dangers in the journey:

> I lift up my eyes to the hills—
> from where will my help come?
> My help comes from the LORD,
> who made heaven and earth.

The dangers included slipping on a rocky path, sunstroke, night threats, and beatings by thieves. When lifting up their eyes to the journey ahead, the pilgrims cry, "Help!"—then trust that the keeper of Israel "will neither slumber nor sleep" (v. 4), that God will shade them by day and protect them by night. The Lord will "keep your going out and your coming in" forever (v. 8). The journey requires letting go of the fear of danger and harm in order to make the pilgrimage. Once the pilgrims arrived safely, they attested:

> If it had not been for Lord who was on our side . . .
> when our enemies attacked us, . . .
> they would have swallowed us up alive, . . .
> Blessed be the LORD,
> who has not given us
> as prey to their teeth.
> We have escaped like a bird
> from the snare of the fowlers; . . .
> Our help is in the name of the LORD
> who made heaven and earth.
> —PSALM 124:1, 2–3, 6–7, 8

Once the pilgrims arrived at the temple site in Jerusalem, prayers of thanks, confession, lament, and praise were offered for God's presence. And in returning home, they took hold of their renewed identity as the people of God, living out their destiny as a nation under God.

Years ago, before leaving on our annual family vacation—the station wagon loaded with baggage and our four children buckled in safety belts—we would pause to read Psalm 121. We called it our traveling song, entrusting our trip to the safety of God's keeping.

In the early 1970s the Taizé community in France became a destination for many young people across Europe and around the world. In 1971 three thousand of them showed up for Easter weekend. The following year thirteen thousand came. And the next year thirty thousand arrived. When I asked one of the brothers why so many came, he replied, "Because we pray." A shrine may not be the only attraction for pilgrims; a community that represents and embraces God's presence may attract them as well. Most young people left Taizé wearing the Taizé cross around their necks. For months afterward they recognized each other on trains and in various public places, where they recalled, shared, and testified to their experiences.

Individuals may have their own particular destinations where they have had mountaintop experiences of recognizing God's presence. They frequently return to these holy places for reminders and renewal. Those places may be found in the remote solitude of natural settings, especially in mountaintop environs; in a busy traffic-laden place; or where joyful or even tragic events have occurred. I like to return to a pew in the choir loft of my home church, where I sat when a powerful sense of call to ministry came over me as a teenager. Many who return to their holy places are reminded that life has been different because of that initial encounter, and they invest anew in greater initiatives. While there, they are reminded of decisions that were truly life changing. They continue to take hold of new visions and commitments that set them on paths that they never would have traveled had it not been for the mountaintop experience.

ODYSSEY

Homer's *Odyssey* is an epic poem depicting the ten-year wanderings of Odysseus, king of Ithaca and Greek leader of the Trojan

War. It took him ten years to reach home after the war. Webster's Dictionary defines *odyssey* as "1: a long wandering or voyage usually marked by many changes of fortune, 2: an intellectual or spiritual wandering or quest."[4] For many people, wandering in the wilderness depicts the spiritual journey. In that wandering, the three movements of letting go, naming God's presence, and taking hold appear, disappear, and reappear. Odyssey is characterized by surprise and the unexpected. A predetermined goal or preferred vision may not materialize, or it may show up in unexpected ways.

Allow me to present a profound personal experience. While recording it in my journal, I named it an odyssey.

The cold, bleak January morning found me hitting the road before dawn, starting a long trek across snow-clad plains for a funeral in a monastery. When I left home, the temperature was minus ten degrees and I had a five-hour drive in front of me. It gave me time to think, and my first thought was, "What in the world are you doing?" I was responding to the news of the death of Father Joe, my spiritual director and friend of several years. Although my first reaction had been one of surprisingly deep sorrow, perhaps deeper than I felt over the loss of my own father, I dismissed the thought of attending the funeral because of the distance and subzero weather. But in the two days following the news, I found tears welling up with every recall of Father Joe.

So at the last minute I determined to go. A strong inner urge impelled me to get on the road, imbuing the journey with a meaning deeper than ordinary travel. The word *odyssey* came to mind. But at that time I had no inkling of what this spiritual quest might be about. Inwardly, I just knew I had to be there. Perhaps the five-hour drive would provide an opportunity to ponder the meaning of the odyssey.

The trip up was filled with memories of the significant relationship I had enjoyed with Father Joe and his religious community. I remembered my monthly visits to their retreat house while living in the vicinity of the monastery, the quiet hours in the library, and the groups I had taken there for conferences. My wife and I had once lived there as guests of the order for one month, entering into the daily prayer life and sharing friendship over meals with the fathers and brothers in the community. And who could forget the quiet conversations with Father Joe in his special spiritual reflection rooms appointed with his own works of art, Native American religious symbols, and favorite music—from Gregorian chant to spirituals? He was a tall, stately man who radiated inner warmth through his smile and the gentle tones of his voice.

Father Joe at one time served as abbot of the order and headed the training for novitiates. His later roles included retreat master, librarian, and spiritual director. He was a scholar, philosopher, priest, theologian, counselor, teacher, and charismatic lover of God and people. He introduced me to the writings of Thomas Merton, John of the Cross, and Madame Guyon, while commending the practice of a series of spiritual methods. But he never failed to say, with a twinkle in his eyes, "It's so simple: it all comes down to love." These memories put me in touch with at least some reasons for being on the road, reinforcing my sense that additional reasons might lie ahead, that more of his legacy might yet be revealed.

Entering the monastery that day, even more than those many previous times, seemed like returning to a spiritual home. The brothers greeted me warmly. Pleasant odors and sounds from the kitchen indicated that a rich and joyous celebration, one befitting a joyful and well-lived life, was being planned. Bishops, priests, sisters from a nearby order where he taught, family, and hundreds of people like me whom he had influenced packed the chapel for a celebration Mass of his faith, life, and ministry. The service was as rich as his life.

At the funeral his community embraced his calling. At the gravesite following the service, the interment concluded with the monks singing a farewell song that they had sung for the burials of their fathers and brothers for seven centuries. They sang it first in Dutch, then twice in English:

May you have a long life.
May you have a long life.
May you have a long life in the Gloria.

The lump this ancient benediction created in my throat was instantly dispelled by a second venerable monastic tradition for which I was totally unprepared. Exuberantly, one monk shouted, "Hip, hip," and the community responded, "Hooray!" Then again, "Hip, hip, hooray!" and "Hip, hip, hooray!"—the final words in Father Joe's last rites. I mused, "Now your life has been offered as the ultimate gift. Rest in peace." Bright noonday sun had pierced the slate-gray January sky.

But a casual conversation across the table at lunch with several of Father Joe's many friends sticks in my mind. We all acknowledged the impact he had on our lives and how that impact could continue to make a difference in our futures. On the five-hour return drive home the next morning, two words loomed large in my thoughts: *odyssey* and *mantle.* My favorite prophet, Elijah, came to mind. His experience of the "still small voice" prompted him to take definitive actions—one of which was to place his own mantle over the shoulders of his successor, Elisha. Those of us who made extra effort to gather at this funeral somehow had an impression that we were to carry Father Joe's mantle. Could this have been the meaning of my odyssey? Arriving back home, I realized that this journey had indeed been an odyssey that deepened my own sense of God-given purpose.

In rereading this journal account some years later, I see more clearly the ebb and flow of letting go, naming God's presence, and taking hold. Sacrificing time and effort to make the journey and saying goodbye to an important spiritual friend called for letting go. God's presence was embraced by a community of faith that joyfully entrusted Father Joe to God's eternal care. Those of us whom he influenced took hold of a new cloak for ministry. The eternal rhythm continued to beat on.

GROUP FORMATION

Beginning in the 1960s many church leaders became interested in small groups. Lay renewal groups like Faith at Work, the Pittsburgh Experiment, Yokefellows, Lay Witness Missions, and the movements of charismatic renewal promoted and resourced them. Informal support and growth groups proliferated in the church and in the culture with the advent of the human potential movement. Those of us who actively worked to promote small group formation saw small group initiatives birth, prosper, and decline—and finally die out.

Wanting to understand small group dynamics and their implication for church development, the Institute for Church Renewal in Decatur, Georgia, focused a three-year effort on small group formation and cultivation in order to prepare leaders for these groups.[5] We found that small groups go through distinct and predictable stages of development. In the early formation stage, participants engage in sharing, listening, self-disclosure, and trusting. Folks tend to say, "Isn't it wonderful how alike we all are!"

As the groups continue to meet, members discover they are not all alike. They carry differing expectations about what the group should be and become. Moreover, they begin to doubt the wisdom and capacity of the leader to hold them all together. This stage of disillusionment surfaces hidden expectations and gives rise to discomfort and conflict.

Dietrich Bonhoeffer, in *Life Together,* refers to the "wish dreams" that we bring to community.[6] Those dreams must be shattered in disillusionment, and we must *let go* of them so that the community can receive the grace of Christ. This shattering—coming with the realization that people are never good enough, or smart enough, or resourceful enough to make community happen on their own—is often painful. The monks in monastic settings know this. They know that the better they get to know one another, the more difficult it is to become a community, even in light of centuries of rules and time-honored communal practices. They know that the grace of Christ is the only glue that holds them together. They are brothers because they live in him. Only then can they know that they are a community by gift—not because they have earned it or constructed it. The stage of real birth announces the gospel grace of Christ's presence.

The final stage in group development launches the participants into taking hold in commitment. In mutual covenant, the whole community pulls together toward a common goal and destiny. Eventually they approach a stage of decline and death—the ultimate letting go. Group members ask, "Who and what will I be without this group?" Nothing earthly lasts forever.

LOOKING AHEAD

In this review of various spiritual practices, we have stepped on a number of spiritual practice stones. With each step, we have uncovered time-honored movements that have been made plain with the rhythmic threefold discipline of spiritual direction—letting go, naming God's presence, and taking hold.

We are now ready to see how the three movements in the rhythm work out in time—as moments in the hour, hours in the day, days in the week, and weeks in the church year. In this chapter, I have used italics to highlight the threefold eternal rhythm within each practice. In the next chapters, your sensitivity to them will allow you to recognize the rhythm yourself. The spiritual DNA for this book has been established!

CHAPTER 2

The Rhythm of Spiritual Formation in Time

The rhythm of spiritual formation is embedded in the discipline of spiritual direction and illustrated in widely varied religious practices. As a prelude to discovering how our own church stories connect to the larger story in the seasons of the church year, let's explore how expressions of the three movements—letting go, naming God's presence, and taking hold—take place within various time frames. These appear in (1) the moments of a worship hour, (2) the hours of the ordinary day, (3) the days of the week, and (4) the seasons of the church year.

IN THE MOMENTS OF A WORSHIP HOUR

Regular attendees and visitors alike probably experience more clusters of intense emotional and spiritual moments in congregational worship than during any other single hour of the week. Participants carry both individual and communal stories of the week into the worship service, which like the narrow neck of an hourglass, functions as a concentrating force for examination, reflection, and redemption. During the next week, those stories become intertwined with new unfolding stories.

Think of the times and ways you have been moved in a service of worship—to tears, laughter, awe and wonder, memories, or a sudden insight. If an electronic device were placed in every worshiper's soul to record these special moments and then flashed all of the responses onto a giant screen, how would letting go, naming God's presence, and taking hold register? This could provide a fascinating picture.

When I asked a group of leaders from a Stanley, Kansas, church to identify a story that was significant in the worship life of their church, they all immediately nominated the same event. Then they proceeded to tell this story: In their most recent Christmas Sunday worship service, the six-year-old son of the choir director sang a solo with the adult choir. He was a hit. All the church members knew him and loved him. He sang his solo with clarity, his angelic face beaming grace and innocence. For the whole congregation, this was a moment of taking hold—so congruent with the themes of love, joy, and peace of the Christmas season. This beautiful picture was shattered when, at the close of the solo, the butterflies in his nervous little stomach decided to visit the congregation, and he vomited onto the chancel floor. How awful. How embarrassing. What a shame! Everyone identified with his letting go and suffered vicariously with him in holy horror. But this sudden second change in the mood of the moment was followed by a third one, which was even more powerful and moving. His father rushed from the choir, lifted the boy into his arms, and hugged him for several minutes as the congregation watched and empathized. What a moment! Time stood still as tears flowed in testimony to God's ever-present love and grace.

Your account of a moment or a series of moments may not be so dramatic or filled with suddenly changing fortunes, but various worship practices can still affect you in both predictable and unpredictable ways. The typical worship service invites the practice of letting go, brings the worshiper to the heights of God's presence, then introduces ways to take hold by responding to God's Word. Look at your own familiar worship order—whether a formal liturgy or informal one—and you will see this rising and falling rhythm. Let's walk through them in a typical hour-long service.

Letting Go

Congregations worship in a variety of ways: formal or informal, following a liturgy with read or impromptu prayers, and traditional organ-accompanied hymns or band-accompanied praise songs. The order of service may be printed in great detail, screen prompted, or simply understood by all. Lyle Schaller, a popular researcher and writer on congregational development, commented in a newsletter about his observation of worship orders in California evangelical churches: they sing, they preach, they pray. Therefore, no matter how formal or informal the worship service may be, the three movements of spiritual formation can be identified. Let me describe how that happens in a typical mainline Protestant service that follows a structured liturgy.

In this gathering, we are ushered out of a world of busy activity into a time and space that calls for centering. Surrounded by symbols and other reminders of a grand tradition, we find our attention is drawn into holy and gracious space. A water-filled baptismal font reminds us that we are set apart for life with God in community with others and have made a commitment to ministry. If the font is located at the entrance, we can touch the water and make the sign of the cross on our forehead. Bowing before the cross, the altar, an image of Christ, or a beautiful icon invites a humble spirit. The accompanying music draws us into a different world, different from what we may have heard on the radio or TV during the week. Some churches, having researched the radio stations their members listen to during the week, may offer similar music to help worshipers make the transition into worship. Either way, while settling in, we open ourselves to a new word and a new experience.

The welcome may be extended verbally by old friends or with a smile that says, "It's good to see you here." One pastor testified that placing official greeters in the parking lot was the most effective welcoming practice in his church. Greeters not only welcomed strangers with a word and a smile but also took the time and effort to personally usher them to a nursery, classroom, restroom, refreshment area, or worship space. Recipients of this hospitality were able to release their anxiety about being in an unfamiliar facility among a crowd of strangers.

Whether our church's gathering space buzzes with chatter or hushes in silence, we settle in and prepare to be in God's presence. At some point a worship leader welcomes all—members and visitors alike. Visitors may be introduced by name if they wish. One pastor reinforces the welcome by telling visitors that their presence is their gift. They do not need to put money in the offering plate unless they choose to give cash for the needy.

The call to worship draws congregants into a humble worshiping frame of mind—perhaps with a scripture passage such as, "O come, let us worship and bow down. Let us kneel before the LORD, our Maker, for he is our God" (Ps. 95:6–7)—leaving no question why we are there and who gets the attention. We are drawn outside ourselves.

The opening hymns of praise focus attention on the attributes of God as a loving creator and provider. Hymns and psalms call us to relinquish our own agendas—at least for a while. Helen Lemmel's 1922 gospel song invites the worshiper to

> Turn your eyes upon Jesus.
> Look full in his wonderful face.
> And the things of earth will grow strangely dim,
> In the light of His glory and grace.

Opening prayers of invocation and confession powerfully tug at the baggage we bring to worship. Confession of sin addresses the wrongs we have done, both individually and corporately, that we release to God. In informal house church liturgies, admitting how we are may include acknowledgments of weariness, fear, sorrow, and frustration. The assurance of pardon announces the good news of release and forgiveness. Following that announcement, in some traditions worshipers pass the peace, offering more than a casual greeting. Passing the peace, mediated by the body of Christ, extends the grace of God. Letting go has just happened in a reassuring environment.

Naming God's Presence

The Word of God read and preached, along with the sacrament of the Lord's Table, becomes the fulcrum or hinge upon which worship services turn. For Protestants, God's own presence comes alive in the reading and preaching of the Word—Holy Scripture—and in the sacrament of the Lord's Supper. For Catholics, in the Mass Christ's presence is realized as bread and wine are blessed, then broken and poured. Without splitting theological hairs in this book, suffice it to say that both traditions stress the fact that God is present in worship, and they name and celebrate that presence at this high point of the service.

Taking Hold

Good proclamation holds the storied tradition in one hand and contemporary narratives in the other, inviting the hearer to respond to God's Word. Historic or contemporary creeds, along with scriptural affirmations, can be recited in unison as a way of saying what we believe and affirming our faith. These are sometimes supplemented by individuals' public testimony to their experience of God's grace and a report of service they may have conducted in God's name.

An invitation to embrace faith in Christ or to commit to a particular path of discipleship offers the worshiper another opportunity to respond. Scripture always extends an invitation. That happens in preaching and also in creative Bible study methods.

Walter Wink, a professor at Auburn Theological Seminary, New York City, offers a way to respond to Scripture via his Transforming Bible Study process. He asks three questions: What does it say? What does it mean? and, What would it be in me? The third question invites a response.[1] Another informal method of studying the Bible asks, What does the text say? What strange twists does the reading take? and, What does the text invite in us? Both of these Bible study methods call for taking hold, as does good preaching.

In the rite of baptism, the new believer renounces sin and evil, rejecting the powers that poison and imprison. The old ways of life fall away while a new way is embraced. An ancient stone baptismal pool, found on a hilltop in Greece, faces east and contains steps that lead down into the waters. The new believers in the early Christian church received their final instruction during the period of Lent. On Easter morning, catechumens' old robes were removed, and they stepped into the water—indicating personal death to and drowning of sin. They were baptized into new life in Christ. As they stepped up eastward, toward the rising morning sun, the elders of the church placed new robes over them. (Thus we have the tradition of new clothes at Easter.) Putting off the old clothes symbolizes a form of letting go. Putting on new clothes symbolizes taking hold.

Moments When Time Seems to Stand Still

Although many orders of worship focus attention to God's Word at the middle of the service, the worshiper may become aware of that presence at any time or within any practice in the service. Worship—like life itself—conjures surprises. God cannot be boxed into a particular time or exercise. A moment of awareness may be brief and fleeting, or it may tarry for a while to be savored. While experiencing such awareness, time may seem to stand still.

For years I have related my own powerful experience of being called to ministry as a sixteen-year-old. The calling involved an old church clock. Several years ago I was invited to lead a retreat for Disciples of Christ and United Church of Christ ministers. I brought the clock with me and opened the retreat by telling my story about the clock and then invited participants to tell some aspect of their own stories.

During the dedication of the new church in 1952, I was seated with the choir and had a clear view of the clock, one of the few items from the old church that had been brought into the new one. The visiting preacher that night was a former pastor who had returned from Chicago to deliver the sermon. He focused on God's desire for human lives dedicated to God's purpose—not just brick and mortar. At about 9:35 the old clock stopped. Thinking he had plenty of time, the guest preacher began to apply this message to different groups in the church—elders, parents, teachers, and finally "young men for the gospel ministry." His words seemed to be directed at me. I squirmed in my seat. I noted the clock and knew that he was scheduled to catch the 10:10 p.m. Denver Zephyr train to return home, so I hoped he would end his message soon. After he finally ended his sermon, he invited people to come forward and kneel for the closing prayer. I resisted and sat glued to my seat. I could not wait to get out of there. (Yes. He did catch the train!)

I left the dedication service in a hurry and went out to watch my buddies play in a Junior Legion baseball game but could not develop interest in the game. I went home to get something to eat, thinking that I could eat off this gnawing feeling. That did not help, either. Finally, I went off to bed thinking I could sleep it off. But to no avail—tossing and turning into the middle of the night—when I finally said, "OK, God, if you want me to be a minister, I will be one." I immediately went to sleep. The next morning a new young minister took several of us to a youth conference, where the same message was repeated and confirmed. At the close of the conference I publicly related the calling and my decision to say yes.

Across the years, whenever I returned to visit my home church, I noted that the same old clock was faithfully keeping good time. Forty-five years after the dedication event I returned to my home church to discover the old clock was missing, having been replaced by a new one. After the service I inquired about the clock and was told that it no longer worked and had been placed in a back closet. Knowing my story, the elders voted to let me have the old clock. It hangs in my office to this day fixed at 9:35 as a reminder of my calling.

When I finished telling this group of ministers about the clock that stopped, a sudden question arose. Did the clock actually stop? Or did time stand still for me? Wow! What if I had been deceiving myself for fifty years? But which is the greater miracle and mystery: a clock ceasing to work in the middle of a sermon, or time standing still for me while I processed what I needed to let go of and take hold of within this moment of God's powerful presence?

I now have new insight into several Old Testament accounts of when time seemed to be standing still. In one of its battles with hostile neighbors, Israel thought the sun stood still so that they could prevail in the fight (Josh. 10:12–14). A short time was filled with so much dynamic activity that it seemed to have been very long.

Moses's attention was turned aside for a moment to contemplate a burning bush that was not being consumed by fire. In that poignant moment, he was aware of the presence of the great "I AM," resisted God's call to deliver a suffering people from Pharaoh's hand in Egypt by offering multiple excuses, and finally agreed to go with God's help (Ex. 3:1—4:20). Who knows how many minutes, hours, or even days were packed into that moment? Time stood still in that sacred space.

Many can testify to sacred moments in an hour of worship and beyond. Look to your own experience. What do your significant moments look like? If we added them together and projected them onto a giant screen, we would be amazed at their variety and the way they cluster around the eternal rhythm of letting go, experiencing God's presence, and taking hold.

IN THE HOURS OF THE DAY

"When does your day begin?" I like to ask seminar participants this tricky question. People respond, "When the alarm goes off . . . When the dog licks my face . . . When the sun lights my room . . . When the kids leave for school . . . When I sip my first cup of coffee . . . When I splash my face with water . . ." All of the responses tend to be associated with rising from bed and beginning daily routines. I remind them that in a Genesis account of creation, the conclusion of each day of creation is punctuated with the statement, "And there was evening and there was morning, the first day. . . . And there was evening and there was morning, the second day. . . . And there was evening and there was morning, the third day," and so on (Gen. 1:5, 8, 13, 19, 23, 31). The day begins at evening. What an inspiring thought! But wait a minute. Perhaps it is not so revolutionary. Then we remind ourselves that the Jewish Sabbath begins at sundown on Friday.

In our culture we see the day beginning with morning, when we rise with much energy to face the new day. As the day wears on, the energy wanes until we collapse, sometimes in exhaustion, into bed. Imagine a new way of looking at the rhythm of the day. What if we begin the day at evening by resting in God? Then we rise out of that rest in the morning to participate with God in the work of the day.

The monastic tradition organizes daily life around a rhythm of daily prayers, which may occur as many as seven or as few as two times a day. Within any scheme of prayer, evening and morning offer the two hinges on which daily prayer turns. For this discussion, we will consider four—evening prayer, night prayer, morning prayer, and day (or noon) prayer. This rhythm dramatically expresses the basic movements of spiritual formation—letting go, naming God's presence, and taking hold.

Evening

Evening prayer invites us to examine the experiences and attitudes of the day, considering the ways we have spent our energy—for good or ill. We revisit the decisions we have made on the paths traveled or less traveled. We think of relationships with others and whether they have been life enhancing or life depleting. Emotions generated during the day surface, linger, and nag at us. What will we do with these reflections? The apostle Paul advises us not to let the sun go down on our anger. These emotions are to be released, lest they eat at us and gnaw us to death. We pay a price for holding onto resentments and other feelings, such as of guilt or failure. Even good unfinished business can steal our energy. So relinquishment becomes the order of the day. We can let go of the residue of the day, entrusting it to God for God's touch of forgiveness, grace, and healing. We can offer thanks for ways in which God has blessed us in the course of the day.

In some profound way, relinquishing at sundown offers a way to prepare for death itself. I recall an interview with a Trappist monk. He was asked to state his purpose in life and responded, "My purpose in life is to prepare my life to be the most beautiful gift that I can create, then offer it to God in my death." For him, death was not a tragic snatching away of precious life but rather an offering—a way of ultimately letting go.

Listen to the familiar children's prayer: "Now I lay me down to sleep. I pray the Lord my soul to keep. And if I die before I wake, I pray the Lord my soul to take." What a way to start the day—by placing one's soul before God for safekeeping.

The psalmist affirms a similar theme. In Psalm 4, a night psalm, David sings, "I will both lie down and sleep in peace; for you alone, O Lord, make me lie down in safety." The refrain of a Psalter setting translates it, "In the night I can take my rest. You alone keep my life secure!"

The grand old evening hymns invite the same prayer. I love these hymns and regret that the concentration of attention on morning worship and the absence of evening worship in most congregations reduce the number of evening hymns to a small section of most hymnbooks. Note the few remaining titles: "Day Is Dying in the West," "Now the Day Is Over," "All Praise to Thee, My God, This Night," "Day Is Done," "Abide with Me," "Now, on Land and Sea Descending," and the third-century hymn, "O Gladsome Light" (*Phos Hilaron*). These evening hymns invite us to let go and entrust daily life into God's hands, and usually one verse speaks of relinquishment in death itself.

A significant experience with the evening hymns for me took place in a gazebo at a conference center. Eight of us had gathered for a training session. (I have a photo over my computer of us in that gazebo.) At sundown we took hymnbooks to the gazebo and sang all of the evening hymns a cappella while sitting in a circle. None of us was prepared for the impact of blended sound and word. The benches were positioned around the eight sides. The roof consisted of eight pie-shaped panels, each becoming a sounding board. While singing, we heard voices of the other seven who were seated on both sides of us, those across from us, and the mixed sounds of all of us echoing off of the ceiling—truly a communal "surround sound" that penetrated our hearts.

Listen to an example of the prayers in these hymns, typically revealed in "Day Is Done."

Day is done, but love unfailing
Dwells ever here;
Shadows fall, but hope, prevailing,
Calms every fear.
God our maker, none forsaking,
Take our hearts of Love's own making,
Watch our sleeping, guard our waking,
Be always near.

Eyes will close, but You unsleeping,
Watch by our side;
Death may come, in love's safekeeping,
Still we abide.
God of love, all evil quelling,
Sin forgiving, fear dispelling,
Stay with us, our hearts indwelling,
This eventide.[2]

Night Prayer

Nighttime brings us to God's presence not only in the blessed
assurance of going to sleep but also in the process of distilling
spiritual wisdom while sleeping through the night. I met a young
Jewish mystic while hiking on a mountain trail, and we engaged
in conversation about nighttime. He said that in Jewish tradition,
the night divides into two parts. The first part tends to be restless
and fitful, a time when the mind and spirit try to make sense out
of the day's experiences or the next day's challenges. I have experienced that while working on a building or remodeling project. I
have awakened in the middle of the night, measuring in my mind
whether to move a wall one-half inch this way or that! The unre-
solved issues seek resolution. Once that has been accomplished, I
can return to sleep. My new friend on the trail mentioned a story
from tradition regarding King David. David purportedly hung his
lyre over his bed at night. Then in the middle of the night when
the cool sea breezes blew through an open window, the instrument would sound, and David would rise to play it and sing praise
to God.

While reading the psalms, I often speculate that they must
have been written between 2:00 and 4:00 in the morning. The
writer has not been able to reconcile the fact that the wicked
prosper and seem blessed while the faithful are victims of injustice, suffering hardship, and poverty. After laying this out and

wrestling with it in light of the great story of God's good creation, the call of Abraham's people, deliverance from slavery, the gift of a land, and the establishment of a nation with a center for worship, the psalmist finally resolves the matter by resting in God's faithfulness and attesting to God's grace in prayer and praise. God's presence in the night comes by way of reflection and leads to wisdom. The last part of the night, according to my young Jewish friend, moves out of a fitful restlessness and light sleep into a deep, trusting sleep.

Psalm 16 expresses that hope in the words from *The Psalter*:

> When in the night I meditate on mercies multiplied,
> My grateful heart inspires my tongue to bless the Lord, my
> guide.
> Forever in my thought the Lord before my face shall stand;
> Secure, unmoved I shall remain, with God at my right hand.[3]

Morning Prayer

Morning prayers thank God for protection and rest through the night and affirm life and our call to ministry. Psalms 4 and 5 hinge on the breaking of morning. Whereas Psalm 4 speaks about resting in God, Psalm 5 offers morning praise. A psalm setting proclaims:

> As morning dawns, Lord, hear our cry.
> O sovereign God, now hear our sigh.
> As first light brings the sun's warm ray,
> Accept our sacrifice of praise.
>
> Your steadfast love shall welcome all
> Who seek your house and on You call.
> O lead us, Lord, in righteousness,
> As through this day Your name we bless.[4]

Some call each morning little Easter, when the rising sun attests to Jesus's resurrection and victory over the bonds of death. This is the time to take hold, celebrate the gift of life, and align oneself with God's purpose and initiative in the world. Morning prayer often includes words such as *call, vocation, discipleship, ministry, purpose, plan, strategy, opportunity, giftedness,* and the like. The wounded world and needy people come to mind and trigger compassion. We lift them before God in prayers of intercession. Morning prayers become taking-hold prayers in the rhythm of spiritual formation.

Day Prayer

Awareness of God's presence can be claimed not only in the night hours via reflection but also in a second way—through the activity of the day hours. Whereas night prayers are passive, day prayers are active and engaging. The Jesus Prayer, attached to the rise and fall of the breath, comes into play. Even while engaging in the day's work, the prayer continues within the subconscious in a subliminal way, whether we think consciously about the prayers or not. Jesus's teaching, "When you do it unto the least of these, you have done it unto me" (Matt. 25:40, my paraphrase), attests to daily work as an arena of God's presence. The brief pause at noonday to offer thanks and praise—often at mealtime—becomes a prayer of presence, as do mutterings under one's breath, "God help me, God show me, God lead me, God sustain me, or God give me patience." They testify to the presence of the indwelling Spirit.

The pictures of Brother Lawrence surrounded with his pots and pans remind us how immediate God's presence can be in the mundane activities that sustain life and community. But the ongoing work of hospitality, reconciliation, holiness, justice, generosity, and peacemaking offer equally important arenas for practicing God's presence in the work of the day.

Picture the hours of the day as a twenty-four-hour clock:

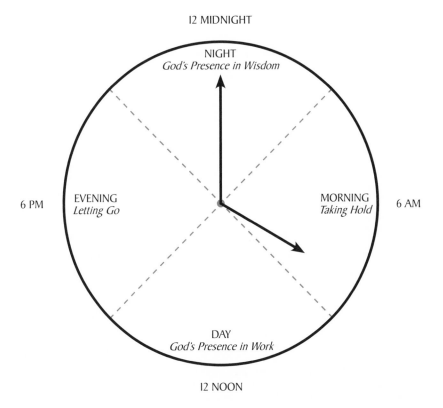

IN THE DAYS OF THE WEEK

Often program-oriented congregations do not design their weekly schedule with an eye toward the divine rhythm of letting go,
naming God's presence, and taking hold. They acknowledge that
worshipers go forth from worship to serve and that this is the ultimate manifestation of aligning with God's purpose and work
in the world. But if we look closely at practices from church history and tradition, we will discover ways to plan particular days
within any given week so that they reflect the rhythm of spiritual
formation.

Imagine my surprise when this Midwesterner's first congregation in Pennsylvania required the pastor to plan and conduct "preparatory services" during the week preceding Holy Communion. I discovered a grand and rich tradition related to the use of communion tokens. The practice was recommended by John Calvin, the father of the Reformed Faith and subsequent Presbyterian Church, to prevent unworthy persons from participating in Holy Communion. The Reformed Church in France, the Dutch Reformed Church, and Presbyterians in Scotland picked up the practice. In those days communion was served only several times a year, and participants were required to receive prior instruction by the elders, which included self-examination to determine participants' worthiness to receive the bread and cup. When they had taken adequate steps to prepare, they received a communion token. Communion was served at numbered tables. Participants placed their communion tokens in the hands of serving elders in exchange for the bread and cup.

The old Presbyterian churches of Pennsylvania had once used the communion tokens extensively, as did the congregation I was serving. Although this old United Presbyterian Church no longer used the tokens, they did observe the holdover practice, preparatory services. (Metal communion tokens have become valuable objects among antique collectors in Pennsylvania.) The congregation's Scottish forefathers observed the Thursday before communion as a day of fasting. It was a day for personal examination and prayer and concluded with a public service in the evening. So in the congregation I served, on one designated evening—usually Thursday—a service of preparation was held. The service centered on scripture texts and preaching that would facilitate self-examination, confession, and reconciliation, inviting participants to let go in tangible ways. In a similar way, the Wednesday night prayer meeting in evangelical churches serves a role in preparation for Sunday worship. It offers an arena for self-examination and opportunity to release to God whatever may block eventual awareness of God's presence.

Holy Week itself presents a model for the rhythms of spiritual formation for all weekly patterns. It begins with celebrating Palm Sunday and anticipating the passion of Christ. The whole last week of Christ's life in Jerusalem was surely one of passion. Today most liturgies begin with the upbeat sounds and themes of Palm Sunday but quickly move to the more somber moods of Holy Week—relinquishment and death. Disciplines of self-denial practiced during Lent now intensify through the week. Maundy Thursday services may be enriched by table meals with an eye to the Jewish Seder service or house-church-type love feast. Feet washing, breaking bread, holy embracing, and kneeling all forge a humble spirit. Good Friday services, with eyes to the cross and readings of the Passion story and held in a dark sanctuary that has been stripped to simplicity, empty the worshiper of pride and haughtiness.

The ecumenical Taizé community in France uses a compressed Holy Week model to plan their weekend services for the many nonchurched or nominally churched young people who come there for a retreat. Friday evening services incorporate a practice the community discovered in Eastern Europe during the Cold War and introduced to the Western world. They call it "prayers around the cross." Small groups of Eastern European Christians would gather on Friday evening in homes. Kneeling at a large cross positioned horizontally about sixteen inches off the floor, they left their pain, their concerns, and the world's pain at the cross. Then they went to worship the following Sunday morning to celebrate the gospel of release and healing. Those who attend the Friday evening Taizé service often spend up to two hours kneeling, singing in Latin, and praying—bringing the pain of the world to that cross.

One church I served picked up the idea, inviting folks to come to the church at any convenient time on Good Friday. A large cross had been laid in the chancel and those who attended maintained a covenant of silence while coming and going. They wrote their concerns, sins, and awareness of the world's pain on sticky note pads and stuck the pages to the cross. Over the hours, the cross began to look heavy from the accumulating notes. Then on Easter morning the cross was stripped and emptied of its burden. The notes were replaced by a white grave cloth draped over the cross. This visually compelling experience proved to be a powerful practice and a self-emptying prelude to the Easter celebration of the risen Christ.

Another adaptation of a Holy Week model can be found in Upper Room Ministries' Five Day Academy of Spiritual Formation. My friend Danny Morris, formerly on the staff of Upper Room, shared that program's history. Those who birthed it wanted to offer Protestant Christians a taste of the rhythms and practices from the monastic tradition, so they designed a process that would include community, worship, silence, and instruction. In experimenting with a weekly structure, they came upon a design that has proven itself in both the two-year academy and its five-day counterpart. A Five Day Academy I attended in March 2008 in Nebraska remained true to this original DNA. The worship themes over the days illuminate six aspects of Christian liturgy. A worship handout from that event describes the themes this way:

Sunday: Gathering
As people united in Christ, we come together from a variety of geographic locations and life experiences to form a community of hospitality in this place. Following the example of St. Benedict, we greet one another as we would greet Christ, and we anticipate that we will be blessed.

Monday: Prayer
We bring our hopes, fears, longings, sadness, and joy to God in corporate prayer. We unite our prayers with those of all people throughout time, opening our hearts and imaginations to the beauty of God's reign.

Tuesday: Lament and Confession
Without turning away, we look at the sadness, violence, senseless destruction, and self-centered cruelty that are present around and within us. We join our tears with those of all who suffer and we tell ourselves the truth of the violence resident in our own hearts. As we enter this valley of the shadow of death we pray, *Kyrie Eleison. Lord, have mercy.*

Wednesday: The Peace of Christ
Remembering that Jesus gives his disciples greater peace than that which the world gives, we greet one another with this peace. . . . We open ourselves and our relationships to the healing and reconciliation found in this place.

Thursday: Table Fellowship
Gathering at the Eucharistic table is at the heart of Christian community. In this meal we are united with others around the world. . . . We discover Jesus' generous and radical hospitality and we are challenged to invite the stranger and the outcast into our lives.

Friday: Sending Forth
Having been nourished and refreshed by our gathering and the presence of Christ with us, we go into the world. We carry with us the love of God and the life-giving hope of healing grace. We offer these treasures of our faith to all whom we meet along the way.[5]

I invite you to reread this weekly order and identify the movements of the divine rhythm within it. Then reimagine a potential weekly rhythm for your own congregation or parish that would reflect the divine movements. It may revolutionize the way you design your church program calendar.

The aspect of sabbath rest in the rhythm of each week should not be neglected or minimized. Our fast-paced social and work life can squeeze rest out of our schedules. To name and celebrate God's presence invites us to rest intentionally in God for an extended time each week, as well as in the hours of the night. We do not want to get caught up in the legalisms of a sabbatarian culture, but we need to find patterns that work for us in a modern culture. After all, even God rested from all God's work on a special, holy day.

Having walked through the eternal rhythms in spiritual practice, the moments of the hour, the hours of the day, and the days of the week, we are now ready to move to the weeks in the seasons of the church year. We will ask, what is the season of a particular personal or communal story? Then we can attach that story to a season of the church year, mining it for wisdom that can enhance our own spiritual formation and mission.

IN THE SEASONS OF THE CHURCH YEAR

The eternal rhythms of spiritual formation can be seen in the seasons of the church year. The Christian church year is marked by three long-standing primary festivals: the celebrations of Christmas, Easter, and Pentecost. The Jewish community also ties its religious festivals to designated months of the year as they tell and retell their salvation story—of exodus out of slavery in Egypt, wandering in the wilderness, and possessing a promised land. Passover was observed in the month of Nisan (March–April), the first month in the Jewish postexilic ecclesiastical calendar. Passover roughly corresponds with Christian Passion and Easter observances. The festival of unleavened bread, coinciding with the barley harvest in the fall, also came to be closely associated with Passover. The absence of yeast reminds God's people of the hasty flight from Egypt.

For Christians, holy days and seasons create sacred space in the cycle of the year that can be used as a teaching tool for children and newcomers to faith—and indeed, for deepening personal faith as well. The seasons of the church year tell the story of the life of Christ and God's redemptive work in the world. They also tell the story of the church, the people of God. Timeless stories from tradition offer a way for us to connect our own personal and group stories to a larger picture and mine them for wisdom from a deep and rich history of faith. When we make those connections, we will be drawn into the divine rhythm of letting go, naming God's presence, and taking hold. We will also see how our own stories both reflect and can be interpreted in light of the seasons of the church year.

Taking their cue from a world that thrives on imitation, congregations often shift from one program emphasis to another without taking an in-depth look into their own unique pilgrimage. But when they claim their own stories and work with them in relation to the seasons of the church year, they connect those stories to an ongoing story of God's mighty acts. In so doing, they rediscover the reason for the church's existence. Telling and reflecting on seasonal stories ground the church in an identity as the people of God on a pilgrimage of faith. Personal stories may be drawn from family, vocation, volunteering, or interpersonal and social relationships. Communal stories may be drawn from mundane or exciting matters of church life—board meetings, pastoral searches, program and staff appraisal, officer training, stewardship campaigns, building projects, mission trips, parties, program initiatives, and the like. When stories drawn from these and other events become the congregation's shared lore for reflection and celebration, the church will find itself traveling an exciting journey with God.

W. Paul Jones, a retired United Methodist professor at Saint Paul School of Theology, Kansas City, and now associated with a Roman Catholic Trappist order in Missouri, drew my attention to the church year in an article he wrote for an Upper Room journal for spiritual formation. He pointed out the similarities between the seasons of Advent-Christmas-Epiphany and those of Lent-Easter-Pentecost: "I am intrigued by the pervasiveness of joy as a theme both in Scripture and in the church's traditions. It is no surprise, then, that the church year itself is structured by triads of joy. Whether the triad is that of Advent-Christmas-Epiphany, or Lent-Easter-Pentecost, the basic Christian rhythm is disclosed: joy as yearning, joy as delight, and joy as sharing."[6]

Where Jones sees two repeating triads, I see three in the eternal rhythm centered around three primary Christian festivals—Christmas, Easter, and Pentecost. Christmas is a festival of the Father who gives in love. Easter is a festival of the risen Son who by grace sacrificed his life for all. Pentecost is the festival of the Holy Spirit, who indwells believers with power. The major festivals name and celebrate a trinitarian presence and formative trinitarian spirituality. Each of these three festivals has a prelude and a postlude as well, so that each of the three triads corresponds to the three movements of spiritual formation—letting go, naming God's presence, and taking hold. Advent is like Lent is like pre-Pentecost in our letting go while waiting and yearning. Christmas is like Easter is like Pentecost in our naming and celebrating God's presence. And Epiphany is like Eastertide is like Ordinary Time, the season after Pentecost, in our taking hold by proclaiming and sending. Putting these triads together, we discover what I call the waltz of the gospel—one, two, three; one, two, three; one, two, three. The journey of faith, which may be taken in one or more of the seasons, becomes a lilting waltz, not a rigid march. The unfolding narratives in our life connect with the church seasons and the eternal rhythms of the gospel. Figure 2.2 illustrates the three festivals with their accompanying rhythmic triads.

In addition to learning from the structure and movements of the church year itself, the accompanying lectionary readings from the Old and New Testaments invite us to look inward to our own stories. When we look at them, we see that our stories can be

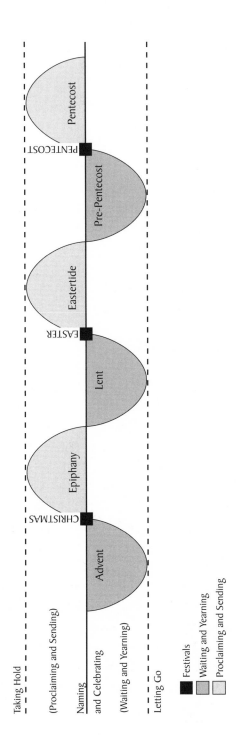

Fig. 2.2. The Rhythmic Triads of the Church Year

associated with various seasons of the church year regardless of when they occurred in the calendar year. Recognizing the eternal rhythms in the movements in the church year can help us coordinate our dance steps with the music of the ages—at any location on the dance floor.

Some may object to placing so much narrative freight on the overloaded train of church seasons, observing that fewer folks understand or are in tune with the church seasons these days. Objectors may even call it a relic of a Christendom whose days are over. They point to the growing popularity of churches that do not follow prescribed lectionary readings, preferring series of topical sermons. For them, lack of familiarity with the church seasons may limit the seasons as a useful structure for prompting and reflecting on their stories. But I see an increasing interest in ritual and the church year, even among nonliturgical churches, and regular use of the accompanying lectionary readings in mainline Protestant denominations.

I believe even the apathetic or marginally active church member, along with new seekers, who push Christmas and Easter worship attendance to the top of the charts, could connect their lives to the rhythms of the church year. What precedes these festival events and what flows from them? What leads up to and follows Christmas? What leads up to and follows Easter? With these questions, we are thrust into the seasons of the church year. I believe that more people than we may presume would be willing to enter the dance. They would welcome the opportunity to connect their own stories to a vital tradition.

The focus of our narrative work engages both personal and communal congregational stories. Several noteworthy efforts have been made to connect stories to the tradition of the church seasons. Linda J. Vogel and Dwight W. Vogel, retired from the faculty of Garrett-Evangelical Seminary, Evanston, Illinois, published a work on how daily life intersects with the church year. They summarize the connection:

When we long for things to be different, when we watch and
   wait,
      we are an Advent people.
When we recognize the presence of the holy in the
   ordinary,
      we celebrate Christmas.
When a sense of the sacramental is broken open to us, and we
   respond by offering our material wealth, our worship, our
   lives and our deaths,
      we live an Epiphany life.
When we wrestle with life and death decisions, seeking to live
   out our baptism,
      we are in Lent.
When saving victory and suffering are closely interwoven,
      we live in resonance with Passion/Palm Sunday.
When death and resurrection become one word, and we are able
   to dance on the gravestones without ignoring them,
      we live as an Easter people.
When the dynamics of our mountaintop experiences are
   uncovered,
      we experience the meaning of the Great Fifty Days.
When we are aware that the Holy Spirit empowers us and sends
   us forth for service, ministry and mission, aware of both the
   diversity and unity of God's people,
      we become Pentecost people.
And when life seems mundane and we put one foot in front of
   the other in order to do what needs doing,
      we are in Ordinary Time.[7]

Although their book accents the personal connections between
experience and the church year, the application can be extended
to communal stories as well.

Several years ago, while presenting a leadership development workshop for teams of congregational board and council

members, I introduced the church seasons as a way to access rich biblical tradition for theological reflection upon their church stories. Following the workshop, a friend, the late Jim Thompson, talked with me about work he had conducted for a DMin program on a similar theme for Sioux Falls Seminary in South Dakota. He had focused on the use of personal stories for spiritual development. He encouraged me to look at his doctoral work and to draw comparisons with my emphasis on communal stories. Jim had worked with several small test groups in two different churches over a two-year span in the early 1990s. Prior to each series of meetings, the group explored a prestudy question: "What biblical stories and/or themes are important to you when you think of Advent, Christmas, Lent, and Easter?" A poststudy question followed the series: "What biblical stories and/or themes are important to you in a new or deeper way in light of our study and sharing?"[8] At the end of the process he concluded, "The participants discovered that the great biblical stories—and their themes that provided the basis for the Christian celebration of those church seasons—were the very recurring stories and themes of their own lives!" Individual testimonies confirmed his observation:

- "I found I could adapt the seasons of the church calendar to my life, which makes it far more meaningful."
- "Learning how we can relate our lives to the seasons of the church is opening an entire new avenue of thought for me."
- "The format and sharing gave me a sense of direction. I, at least, was at a loss as to how to proceed until I saw what path we were to take. I don't suppose I had ever related the happenings in my life to the great events of the church before. In the sense that we have all experienced great joy and great sorrow, it was helpful to be able to relate it to the seasons of the church."

In December 2008 I met with seven people from Westminster Presbyterian Church in Des Moines who had participated in Jim's original groups to see what they remembered from the experience and what the impact might have been. Recent data is important for research projects, but I assumed an experience that had stuck for fifteen years could be even more important. What might the lasting effect be on an individual or a congregation that has related its story to the seasons of the church year?

They reported that they had vivid and lasting memories of their experience. They remembered how close and trusting their group had become. They remembered not only the tears shed in difficult times but also how even those hard times put them in touch with the biblical stories associated with the church year—especially the season of Lent and the dynamics of Holy Week and Easter. They attested to how much more personal their faith had become. They related how the small group experience provided them with an outlet to tell their own stories. The structure of the seasons offered them a way to tell their stories, and the confidentiality in the group invited them to risk laying their stories before others. Their eyes were opened to how they lived out the church year in their everyday experience from Advent to Christmas to Lent and to Easter.

They appreciated the leadership of Jim Thompson, who contributed to the impact. He was skilled at prompting stories and able to help the group connect their own stories to the respective seasons. One member lamented, "This way of working with stories is an important work that not many pastors know."

Had their personal experience of connecting their own stories to the church seasons given them any insight on their journey as a congregation? Yes. They spoke of coming together to remember and grieve the tragic deaths of a beloved pastor and his daughter in a drowning accident—a Lenten connection. They remembered the work of an Alban consultant who worked with their leadership to develop a long timeline of the church's story during one of their developmental transitions—an Advent connection. Corporate connections with the church year abounded.

So yes, making connections between the church seasons and both personal and communal stories had a lasting impact. These members stayed with the church through some rough years. They became involved in the leadership circles of the church. They engaged in various forms of volunteer ministries. And they even found ways to apply their group experience to the church seasons and their professional work settings.

Let's return to the dance floor and enter again into the triads of the waltz. Get ready. Come to attention. Step one—two—three; step one—two—three; step one—two—three. The three-step triads revolve around the festivals of Christmas, Easter, and Pentecost.

CHAPTER 3

The Waltz of the Gospel

Each of the three major festivals of the church year, Christmas, Easter, and Pentecost, offers a subset of three movements—triads of (1) waiting and yearning, (2) naming and celebrating, and (3) proclaiming and sending. Entering into their rhythm can be likened to a waltz that involves three different steps repeated three times over.

Advent, Lent, and pre-Pentecost (the ten days after Ascension Day) are the first step in each triad. (See figure 3.1.) With this lead step, we *wait and yearn* for a hopeful future. The Christmas, Easter, and Pentecost festivals are the second step in each triad. In this follow step, we *name and celebrate* God's presence. And Epiphany, Eastertide, and the ordinary days of the long season of Pentecost are the closing third step of the triad. With this step, we *proclaim and send* people forth with the gospel.

Waltz Steps	Eternal Rhythm	Spiritual Dynamics	Christmas Triad	Easter Triad	Pentecost Triad
1. Lead Step	Letting Go	Waiting & Yearning	Advent Season	Lenten Season	Pre-Pent. Season
2. Follow Step	Naming God's Presence	Naming & Celebrating	Christmas Festival	Easter Festival	Pentecost Festival
3. Close Step	Taking Hold	Proclaiming & Sending	Epiphany Season	Eastertide Season	Ordinary Days of Pentecost Season

Figure 3.1. The Waltz of the Gospel in Stories

THE LEAD STEP: WAITING AND YEARNING

Advent, Lent, and pre-Pentecost are each unique seasons into which a wide variety of congregational and individual stories can be gathered. While waiting and yearning, we find common threads of relinquishment in each. We let go in each season in order to move to a new future—sometimes from our own planning and effort, sometimes from pain and the threat of death, and sometimes from focused spiritual practice.

Waiting and Yearning in Advent

In the season of Advent, we are invited to surface stories of expectations for a future grounded in hope. The stories located in this time reveal dissatisfaction with the present situation and longing for something more. Although the something more may be hard to picture, people's expectations grow. Augustine said, "Our hearts are restless till they rest in Thee."[1] We feel restless for new possibilities that can be fully realized only if God enters the picture. In this time of uncertainty, we may not know what lies ahead. Our yearning could prompt us to plan to move forward toward realizing shared visions—even though the planning process may be tedious, slow, and seemingly unproductive. When we deal with our own stories, both the congregation's and individuals', located in the Advent season, we tend to become impatient and need to know that God is at work, even though we miss the signs. It is a time for letting go and letting God. While waiting and yearning, we search for signs that the new may be around the corner and even prepare ourselves to be receptive to what God may offer. We might ask ourselves the questions:

> What values do we hold that could be projected into a picture
>   of a new future?
> What might we ask of God that we cannot do for ourselves?
> What might a surprise of grace look like?

God acted "in the fullness of time" to send the Son (Gal. 4:4). We often want God to act on our time schedule. But God's timing is usually better than ours. When we look back, we see that God's gifts and graces came at a more appropriate time than we could have masterminded. The testimony of Scripture in the writings of the prophets of Israel and the records of the experiences of Mary, Joseph, Elizabeth, Zechariah, and John the Baptist all indicate that God was not silent. These people of faith waited and yearned—often letting go of personal agendas in order to receive God's gifts.

Within the worship life of congregations, any pastor who has tried to hold off singing Christmas carols during Advent knows the impatience of the people. After all, since Halloween they have been listening to Christmas music while shopping! In the congregations I served, I usually was able to hold off singing the Noels through the first two Sundays in Advent before letting the Christmas carols in. But it is difficult. People don't like to wait and to let go of the immediate need to get into the full music of Christmas.

The same impatience surfaces in the stories of organizational life. Alban Institute president Jim Wind reflected on the waiting period his organization endured over the course of a year of strategic planning. He likened the dynamics of letting go to the Advent season:

> Advent is a time of waiting, though often in this modern world waiting takes the form of inappropriate rushing and excitement. This is not the sort of waiting the Scriptures describe as appropriate to the season. That kind of waiting involves patience, deliberation, careful watchfulness, and turning inward. . . . Our procedures have been gradual and deliberate. . . . Often we felt frustrated, impatient, and stymied—like one sometimes does during a season of sacred waiting. Can't we hurry this process and get to the celebration and the action? Can't we just dive in and tackle new goals? . . . But we had to continually remind ourselves and each other that a planning process does not happen all at once; that, in fact, leaping

ahead to a conclusion almost inevitably misses important stop-ping points along the way. Indeed, there is no real resolution without stops along the way, and meaning is often found as richly in the process as in its conclusion.[2]

A major section of this book tells and reflects upon specific con-gregational stories that are matched to the seasons of the church year. In chapter 4, you will read an extended Advent story of let-ting go from the Holy Trinity Orthodox Church of Overland Park, Kansas.

Waiting and Yearning in Lent

In the season of Lent, we are invited to surface stories that evi-dence waiting and yearning, but their character is very different from those of Advent. Stories of waiting and yearning in Lent and Holy Week become laced with strange mixtures of excitement and fear, success and failure, loyalty and betrayal, affirmation and de-nial, life and death. Jesus's popular Galilean ministry of teaching and healing took a dramatic turn after his mountaintop visit with Moses and Elijah, when God affirmed for the second time that Jesus was a beloved Son. When Jesus returned from the transfigu-ration he found a confused band of disciples frustrated in their own efforts to heal and teach. From that moment he told them of his determination to go to Jerusalem to encounter hostile death threats. "He set his face to go to Jerusalem" (Luke 9:51). (This turning marks the beginning of our Lenten season.) The crowds did not receive him because they did not understand the direction he was heading. And his disciples objected to even the thought of death. His followers waited and yearned—but for a popular crowning of a king as the culmination to glorious ministry. Mat-thew places Jesus's intent to go to Jerusalem immediately after the feeding of the five thousand, where waiting and yearning were ex-pressed by their determination to make him their king. But Jesus disappointed them, inviting them to let go of their illusion. "From that time on, Jesus began to show his disciples that he must go to Jerusalem and undergo great suffering . . . and be killed" (Matt. 16:21). Our Lenten stories are often filled with the same elements of failure, disillusionment, and frustration.

The forty days of Lent, beginning with Ash Wednesday, reflect Israel's forty years' wandering in the desert before entering the promised land. This ancient holy season of self-denial and repentance is rooted in the early church's practice of instructing new adherents in the faith during a period of fasting and before their baptism at sunrise on Easter morning. The whole church came to adopt the practice of fasting during Lent as preparation for celebrating the festival of Easter. The earliest known recommendation that Christians should fast for forty days before Easter comes from a letter written in 330 CE by St. Athanasius, Patriarch of Alexandria, Egypt. By the Middle Ages, fasting was enforced throughout Europe, and innkeepers faced threats of imprisonment if they served meat during the final weeks before Easter.

The Reformers of the sixteenth century deemphasized the season, but in recent years Protestants have renewed their interest and participation in special Lenten programs and liturgies. Palm Sunday, for instance, which used to be celebrated as Little Easter with worshipers waving palms in joyous processions, marks the beginning of Holy Week with a more somber emphasis on Christ's sufferings. Fasting in identification with the sufferings of Jesus becomes an important discipline for spiritual growth while waiting and yearning for Easter life.

The liturgical color for the season of Lent is purple, which characterizes waiting and yearning in the experiences of repentance, suffering, death, relinquishment, brokenness, alienation, abandonment, loneliness, isolation, and conflict. While putting on the color of purple, an individual might ask:

Do I feel like I am in a wilderness?
Am I facing temptation and need help to resist?
Do I see weakness in myself and the need to change?

What do I need to allow to die in me in order to be closer to
    God?
What do I need to confess in order to be rid of guilt?
With what am I struggling and in pain?
Do setbacks and losses eat away at me?
How far have I strayed from God's purpose for my life?
Do I doubt God, myself, others?
From what or whom do I run away and hide?
Does saying goodbye to people and places leave me feeling sad?

A friend and I used to compare notes on what we each were giving
up for Lent or what new spiritual practice we were initiating for
the season. Two years ago my response was, "I am entering che-
motherapy." My chemo treatment started at Ash Wednesday and
continued into the season of Pentecost. I accepted my trips to the
clinic for six hours of chemical injections as a spiritual discipline,
one in which the forces of death were vying with the forces of life.
The chemicals injected into my body were aimed at a nasty tumor
but damaged my hair, digestive process, and good cells. I experienced much "dying unto self" while I awaited the good news of
Easter life.

Congregations struggle, wait, and yearn as well. Betrayals of
trust, posturing, power moves, hidden dirty laundry, and scores of
other life-depleting attitudes and behaviors sap our common life
and call for resolution and healing. The church knows the stories
of Holy Week within its own life. We might ask, "Is it possible to
discover God's presence in the midst of all this stuff?" Denying
the existence of our struggles will only be self-defeating. Lent calls
us to openly and humbly face them and to offer them to God for
resolution. Now letting go gets into the act, repeating the same
movement of spiritual formation that played at Advent. This time
we let go of anything that hides the existence of our shortcomings
and life-depleting behaviors.

The leaders of one church tell their Lenten story: They were
looking for an associate pastor to share leadership ministry with

the senior pastor. After a long search, the committee unanimously recommended that the pastor's wife, also an ordained minister, be called to the position. When her name was presented to the congregation, her nomination failed by two votes. The ensuing embarrassment, mistrust, misunderstanding, and frustration boiled beneath the surface, and the leaders of the church were at a loss to deal with it. The hurt and confusion cut so deep that they hardly knew how to talk about it. It surely was a Lenten story. They yearned to be free of the pain and confusion. To deal adequately with it, the leaders would have to find an opportunity to tell the story together, thereby forming a corporate memory of it. Then they would need to name the dynamics that surrounded and infected the story. They could associate it with the confusion of the Passion story in Lent and Holy Week—interweaving it with biblical stories. Finally, they could let go of resentments and critical judgments—waiting for God to touch their story with grace. When they offer it to God, they could work their way through it in faith, hope, and love.

Lenten waiting and yearning culminates in Holy Week with the devastation of letting go in death. Dread, not God, seems to hold the future. Neither individuals nor congregations can bypass Good Friday. Walking through the valley of the shadow of death is part of the pilgrimage. For congregations, betrayal by a minister, the departure of a beloved pastor, the burning of a sacred building, a church split, an all-consuming conflict, or an overloaded program schedule sounds the death knell. In the midst of death, we yearn for life.

In chapter 5 we will look at the story of two Montana Roman Catholic missions' walk through this Lenten and Holy Week valley of death in discernment about whether to close their doors.

Waiting and Yearning in Pre-Pentecost

Of the nine steps in our threefold waltz of the gospel, the lead step of waiting and yearning prior to Pentecost Sunday is the least emphasized and practiced. Advent and Lenten seasons are much longer. Pre-Pentecost lasts only ten days. It occurs in late spring and early summer when many folks in the Northern Hemisphere move outside for gardens, recreation, and travel. Is it any wonder that some call this time the blind spot in the church year? Church leaders even have difficulty finding a name for it, so we will just call it pre-Pentecost.

When we look closely at the Great Fifty Days between Easter and Pentecost, we see that the first forty were days of Christ's appearing for the purpose of body building—restoring faith, hope, and love in his disciples (Acts 1:1–3). He wanted to send them out with an awareness that he was alive and would live in and through them. Then his ascension marked the beginning of ten days of focused, concentrated prayer in anticipation of the coming of the Spirit. Jesus ordered his disciples not to leave Jerusalem but to wait for the promise of the Father. And he indicated that he would baptize them with the Holy Spirit (Acts 1:4–5). Instead of charging ahead into witness and ministry, the disciples waited, per Jesus's instructions, until the Holy Spirit empowered them.

The faithful 120 people, including many women followers, who gathered, waited and yearned for Christ to come to them in the form of a dynamic spirit. They let go of human impulses to get going. While there, they prayed. They recalled and told stories of their life with Jesus and his teachings. They reflected on their experience with Jesus and saw how it fulfilled a larger sweep of God's activity that had been described in the psalms. And they assumed a posture of discernment when choosing Matthias to replace Judas as one of the twelve disciples. In other words, they intentionally ceased involvement in active ministry in order to engage in centered religious practices. Being still is not easy—especially for active types like Peter. But after these days of waiting, Peter stood up to preach Jesus and interpret the gift of the Holy Spirit.

How might the followers have prayed in that upper room? Jesus gave them two models. The Lord's Prayer itself could have provided enough structure. They may have recalled another, commonly referred to as Jesus's high priestly prayer (John 17). In that prayer, Jesus prays for his disciples who would reunite after his ascension—and even for those who would eventually believe their message. He prays that his disciples may be united, that they may have joy, that they might be victorious over the evil one, and that they might fulfill his mission to the world (John 17:6–19). Prayers for unity, joy, stamina, and success never go out of style!

Contemporary culture devalues waiting as a waste of time and relinquishing self-will as counterproductive for task initiatives. We want to charge ahead and get with the program. Yet Jesus's teachings and church traditions place high value on spiritual practices that call for waiting. In them we will ultimately find our strength in intentional stillness, and our power in what appears to the outside culture to be weakness and foolishness. In waiting we appear to be fools for Christ; yet it is a vital and important step in the waltz of the gospel. Waiting in stillness will usher us into the presence of the Holy One. Individuals testify to waiting's mystery, and congregations that become still in anticipation of the gift of the Spirit will be transformed and empowered. Congregations will want to consider intentional retreats and periods of focused communal stillness that are not designed to produce outward results. Resting in God is reward enough. Quaker churches attest to emergence of wisdom from silence.

In chapter 6 we will tell the pre-Pentecost story of Trinity Church in Omaha, an independent megachurch that entered into intentional stillness after a wrenching period of conflict.

THE FOLLOW STEP:
NAMING AND CELEBRATING GOD'S PRESENCE

In the waltz of the gospel the second step naturally follows the lead step in a smooth, lilting fashion. When our stories have taken us through the anticipatory waters of Advent, the fear and anguish of Lent and Holy Week, and, in pre-Pentecost, the concentration in prayer in response to Jesus's order to wait, we look for God to break into our lives. In looking for God's presence in the context of our own stories, we will name God as a loving giver, a gracious companion who shares our humanity, and one who sends us an indwelling and emboldening Spirit. Signs of God's presence—sometimes obvious, sometimes barely visible, and sometimes mystically veiled—can be discovered through the telling and re-telling of our stories.

God rarely bolts into our lives to suddenly overwhelm us. The first step in the waltz prepares us for the second—the discovery of presence. Eugene L. Lowry, retired preaching professor from Saint Paul School of Theology and a jazz pianist, conducts seminars and presents programs on the roots of the gospel in jazz. Demonstrating the contrast between straight hymns and those that include grace notes, such as we hear in jazz music, Lowry suggests that "God is sneaky." A grace note is played immediately before the main theme note and effortlessly slips our attention to that main note without calling attention to itself. Without the presence of grace notes, we may feel bombarded or overwhelmed with the sudden surge of sound. But grace notes draw us and ease us into the melody.

The seasons of waiting and yearning serve as grace notes that slip us into celebrative melodies that acclaim God's presence as creator, savior, and spirit in the three festivals of the church year. Advent's grace note draws us from longing into the realization of the love of God. A musical setting for Psalm 42 declares, "There is a longing in my heart for you, O God . . . and for justice . . . for mercy . . . for peace." Lent's grace note reveals that even when we die unto ourselves, we yearn for resurrection life. Pre-Pentecost's grace note quiets us with prayer while we wait to be filled by the Spirit.

Grace notes draw us from the lead step of waiting and yearning to the follow step—naming and celebrating God's presence. When we listen to stories of the church, we will see God's presence named in three ways—in the persons of the Trinity. A familiar benediction announces: "Now may the love of God, the grace of our Lord Jesus Christ, and the power of the Holy Spirit be with you." The historic creeds of the church set beliefs into three distinct paragraphs that describe God's presence and activity as Father, Son, and Holy Spirit.

Practical theologians, such as George Hendry of Princeton Theological Seminary, have tried to condense our understanding of the mystery of the Trinity into brief summary statements. Some statements describe the God who is *over* us, the God who is *with* us, and the God who resides *in* us. In their book on servant leadership, Ken Blanchard and Phil Hodges use popular imagery to talk about the Trinity: "As Christians we get three consultants for the price of one—The Father who started life, the Son who lived life, and the Holy Spirit who handles the daily operations of life."[3]

William P. Young, in his best-selling novel *The Shack*, presents God in trinitarian form as a large African American woman, a Middle Eastern laborer, and a small Asian woman. Why has this book become so popular? Its sales mushroomed because of personal recommendations from friend to friend. Readers bring their own pain—real Lenten season-type stories to the book—and find that they can release that pain to the very heart of God. Young presents God's heart through three approachable persons.[4]

The Greek Orthodox Church embodies the DNA of trinity in the very fabric of its common life. I once told a member of that tradition that she thinks in threes. "Of course," she responded. "I am Orthodox!" Orthodox Church leader Michael McKibben applies trinity to the world of management and strategic planning. He suggests that the Trinity parallels *Vision* (conceived mental image of a product), *Word* (the implementation or incarnation of a vision), and *Enthusiasm* (the spirit of joy and capacity to stick with it.) These three comprise a trinitarian construct.[5]

Using trinitarian affirmations to identify God's presence is not based on rational conjecture or wishful speculation. The Trinity is rooted in the very stories that individuals and churches live out from day to day. If we trust our experience and begin with our own stories, we will be led to discover that God has already moved to meet us in those stories.

Naming and Celebrating in Christmas

The Christmas festival, which is celebrated for twelve days, marks the birthday of Jesus of Nazareth. Our attention often centers on the second person of the Trinity—on a baby in a manger. But closer examination reveals that the festival is all about the first person of the Trinity, whom we celebrate with the words of the angels' praise, "Glory to God in the highest!" This eternal and powerful Creator has chosen to visit a people on earth. The much quoted gospel in a nutshell, John 3:16, declares that "God so loved the world that he gave his only Son."

Author Marva Dawn took a cue from a presentation I gave that keyed the church seasons to the three festival triads. In her book, *The Unnecessary Pastor*, she looks at Christmas as a celebration of the Father. "The three high festivals are actually Trinitarian, though most would think there are two celebrations of Christ. It seems to me that we would be able to avoid the overly romantic sentimentalizing of Christmas if we remembered that it is more fully a festival of the Father, the One who gave us the unfathomable gift of his Son. . . . The other two festivals are obviously those of the Son at Easter and the Holy Spirit at Pentecost."[6]

At Christmas we celebrate a loving and giving God, the creator of the universe and lord of history, who chose to be present with us in the incarnation of Jesus of Nazareth. Mary experiences God's presence and celebrates the Mighty One who has helped Israel for generations, according to the promise made to Abraham. Zechariah sings of God's presence while blessing the God of Israel. The angels' song glorifies God in the highest heaven.

We celebrate this loving and giving God when we name wonders in our own lives:

the beauty of the created order around us
the wonder of a child's birth
the birth of movements and ministries
the awareness that "all things work together for good"
 (Rom. 8:28)
the receipt of an unexpected gift
arriving at a place that feels like home
a benefit from waiting
being close together in a special way
new insights from walking a journey
undeserved love
connection to the larger universe and sweep of history
adoption into a family
a *kairos* moment

Ten years ago Ellen Morseth, BVM, my colleague in Worshipful-Work (a ministry for congregational boards and councils to integrate spirituality with administration in their meetings) presented our model for church board leadership around the practices of story, reflection, vision, and discernment to a retreat for three hundred Episcopal clergy in the Boston area. Shortly after the retreat she received a phone call from one of the participants. He asked if she would be willing to work with his parish in a spiritual discernment process related to an important matter for the church. He explained that an old painting, which hardly anyone liked, had bounced from room to room in the church and finally ended up in the attic of the rectory. He found it and suggested that it be appraised to determine the value. The appraisal revealed that it was a sixteenth-century painting of the Madonna and Child, and it eventually sold for 1.2 million dollars at public auction! Now they needed to decide what to do with the money. They did not want this issue to divide the parish, for many already had formed opinions about how the money should be used—to fix the leaky roof, and so forth. In her work with them, Sister Ellen began by inviting them as a group to tell the story of their relationship with the painting. The story unfolded with many twists and turns—among them the church custodian's discovery that a group of boys were preparing to throw darts at it, aiming at the private parts of the holy child in the painting! The church members reflected theologically on the story of the discovery and appraisal of the painting and were able to name and celebrate a giving God. This was an important first step into what would be a full year of spiritual discernment.

Not every church has this kind of good fortune, although many would wish it to be so. When churches look deeply into their own stories—some trivial, some ordinary, and some dramatic—they will see the giving hand of God. They can open the gifts and sing praise to the giver.

Naming and Celebrating in Easter

In the follow step in the waltz of Easter, God's presence is named in a suffering and risen servant. In Jesus, the God of Easter resides with us, knowing and participating in our everyday life of trial, loss, conflict, and testing—yet prevailing. He was tempted in every way we are tested, yet without sin. The apostle Paul offers a picture of a servant Jesus: "Though he was in the form of God, [he] did not regard equality with God as something to be exploited, but emptied himself, taking the form of a slave, being born in human likeness. And being found in human form, he humbled himself and became obedient to the point of death—even death on a cross. Therefore God also highly exalted him" (Phil. 2:6–9a).

We rarely associate death with the presence of God. Yet we walk into this mystery of the valley of the shadow of death with yearning and hope for life. We trust that the promise of Easter life will break into our story. We have shared the sufferings of Christ in Lent and Holy Week. Now we hope for the same presence of Christ in an Easter resurrection story.

What is the season of Easter for us? It is a time of

- joy and happy endings
- seeing the power of God at work through a miracle
- new life—spiritual, emotional, or physical
- ceasing pain, struggle, and loss
- glad reunion with loved ones
- forgiveness, restoring our relationship with God or others
- a second chance
- overcoming doubt
- gaining insight through suffering
- being freed from restraints
- having courage to take risks
- entering the mystery of life through the door of death
- probing new possibilities

Jesus was raised by the power of God. He is risen indeed! He is alive! We know that our sins are forgiven, and we can share eternal life with God after death. The power of sin and death over all creation has been overcome. Our attempt to kill God—to get rid of God by repeatedly saying no to a call—has failed. God pardons and welcomes us. We have passed from darkness to light. That is the good news of the Easter gospel.

Jesus as the servant is present with us in the sacramental breaking of bread and pouring of wine and within his body on earth—the church. So we can mine our church stories for examples of the servant church. Images of the church's role as a sign of God's purpose for the world fill the New Testament letters: for example, God's intention to unify all things in heaven and earth—male with female, slave with free, rich with poor, and so forth. The living Christ chooses to be present to the world through his body, the church. Jesus promised that where two or three are gathered in his name, he will live in their midst.

A member of a small house church had recently gone through a painful rejection in a messy divorce. When she came to the meeting one week, she related her pain, loneliness, and doubt.

She said, "I am so full of doubt that I can no longer believe in God. I want to ask something of you. Will you believe for me? I can't do it on my own anymore." After further discussion, the members of the group agreed to believe for her. They continued to support her through the following weeks in and between meetings. After several months elapsed, she reported to them, "I no longer need for you to believe for me. I can now believe for myself. I want to thank you for believing for me and urge you to continue because it has meant and continues to mean so much!" She realized the presence of Christ through her believing friends. But they also, as a ministering community of faith, came to a deeper and more profound awareness of Christ in their midst. This group danced the waltz of Easter faith—the grace of Christ's living presence.

For individuals to be formed as a community of Christ, their stories of life and death will need to be broken (like bread) and poured out (like wine) within the community rather than hidden in fear or denial. Then the light of Easter presence dawns.

Naming and Celebrating in Pentecost

The follow step in the waltz of Pentecost proclaims the gift of the Holy Spirit to the church. Jesus promised that a comforter would be given to his followers and instructed them to wait. At the end of the harvest, when faithful Jews gathered in Jerusalem to celebrate, the city was full of pilgrims. God chose to grant the gift of the Holy Spirit to them on what we call the birthday of the church. The enthusiasm of the day could only be described as flaming tongues of fire. Peter told the crowds about this Jesus and called them to faith and baptism in Christ's name. Three thousand new believers responded. Peter cited the prophet Joel's declaration that in the last days God would "pour out [God's] spirit upon all flesh" (Joel 2:28–32; Acts 2:17), connecting that prophecy to the events of the day.

In the festival of Pentecost we experience God's presence as God residing in us, making Christ's presence real to us. When we think Pentecost we see red colors, hear new and strange sounds, and dream big dreams. The indwelling Spirit enables the church to dream new visions and equips the church with special gifts with which to follow the dreams.

In looking to our personal and communal stories, where might we discover the presence of an indwelling and empowering Spirit?

- when we have accomplished the impossible
- when our hearts have been "strangely warmed," like the disciples' on the Emmaus road
- when Scripture has come alive with new light and meaning
- when spiritual gifts supplemented our native abilities
- when new visions surfaced
- when we found consolation rather than desolation in our decisions
- when we received the gift of spiritual discernment
- when timing seemed like a miracle
- when communication broke the silence
- when we stuck with a project
- when we maintained enthusiasm in an effort
- when our community seemed glued together despite differences

While observing groups make decisions together, I have seen the Spirit's presence when the whole group comes to a place of accord. Danny Morris, a former program staff member of Upper Room Ministries, described an experience in which a planning group was trying to discern the shape of a new spiritual formation academy. He likened the exploration to that of slowly turning an imaginary prism located in the center of the group. The process proceeded at a patient pace until suddenly light emanated from the prism for all in the circle to see at once. The light came on.

When congregations are invited to share their stories of being moved or touched in a special way or about when they were able to accomplish far more than they had ever dreamed or about when they were emboldened to take firm stands, their stories will testify to the powerful presence of the Holy Spirit.

THE CLOSE STEP: PROCLAIMING AND SENDING

We now come to our third step in the waltz, the close step, in which the church proclaims the good news and sends forth witnesses and workers for the kingdom. In this step we grasp the spiritual imperative to take hold—not just as disciples who follow but also as apostles for a cause that has radically changed us. We come to care deeply about a world that God cares for and are willing to participate with God in fulfilling God's purpose. We can anticipate that new initiatives will flow from all three major festivals, for they are not the end of the stories. Recognizing God's presence carries an accompanying invitation for us to participate in God's work on earth. What might we expect to flow from the grand news of God's love and gift at Christmas? What might we expect to naturally flow from the incredible news of resurrection life at Easter? What might we expect to happen after the tongues of fire of the church's birth at Pentecost? We cannot just pack up and go home from Bethlehem or Jerusalem. So what is next? We are invited to close the dance step triad by taking the third step—taking hold to proclaim good news and to send disciples into the world to create more stories. Those new stories will match up with the seasons of Epiphany, Eastertide, and the ordinary time of Pentecost.

Proclaiming and Sending in Epiphany

Epiphany means "appearing" or "manifestation." The twelve days of Christmas culminate in the day of Epiphany, January 6. It marks the Wise Men's journey to visit the Christ child. Since the magi were from a far away land in the East, their visit required that they cross a number of boundaries to discover that God's love in the gift of Christ was to be for the whole world. Jesus would be introduced to the whole world as a king worthy of honor. Simeon's blessing of Jesus in the Temple confirmed the message the magi would carry—"My eyes have seen your salvation, which you have prepared in the presence of all peoples, a light for revelation to the Gentiles and for glory to your people Israel" (Luke 2:30–32).

In the Western Christian world, the day has been called the Festival of the Magi or the Day of Lights. On the Twelfth Night, preceding the holy day, Christians pray and read the Scriptures the whole night, then celebrate during that first full day of Epiphany. In some cultures, "kings cakes" were baked in testimony to Three Kings Day. Springs and rivers were blessed, and water from them was collected for use in baptisms for the year. The focus of the celebration was that light had come to the whole world. The gospel of Jesus would shine on all peoples, races, and nations. The angels' message of peace on earth and goodwill to all could not be contained in a tiny corner of the world.

The season invites the church to cross over old boundaries to bring the gospel of reconciliation and understanding to alienated peoples, foster spiritual growth, and remind baptized people of their role as Jesus's disciples. The suggested lectionary readings from the Old and New Testaments illustrate where and how boundaries are crossed as the light of Christmas spreads. Jesus's Galilean ministry attests to the good news and healing for all.

Proclaiming good news and taking on new initiatives for ministry in the season of Epiphany leads both individuals and congregations to ask questions such as these:

What is God calling me or us to do?
Who is my neighbor?
How can I minister to others?

How am I sharing God's love?

Where are my growing edges?

What self-imposed boundaries, barriers, or prejudices might
I or we be led to cross in order to hold the light of love for
all peoples?

Perhaps the birth of Dr. Martin Luther King Jr. on January 15, and
the national holiday in his honor, reflects God's provident hand
in the synchronized timing of our national and religious life. That
celebration for racial harmony and justice happens right in the
middle of the Epiphany season. Could that celebration prompt
congregations to examine their own stories to ferret out latent
racism and to take steps to cross over old boundaries?

January and February also offer a ripe time for new programs
and ministries to be introduced in the church. People tend to
think about New Year's resolutions and initiatives. The energy
and effort that has been put into holiday planning and celebrating
now becomes freed up for new ventures. My colleague Bill Van
Loan, a staff specialist for ministries to singles at Arcadia Presbyterian Church in Arcadia, California, identified singles' personal
issues month by month and prepared corresponding programs
and events to meet their needs. He observed that in January people have a sense of hope and optimism. It is a time for goal setting
and fresh ventures. His Bible study and group programs focused
on overcoming, doing, planning, hoping, and mixing. Key theme
words for the season of Epiphany were *light, life, appearing, calling, mission,* and *planting.* His training of group leaders for the
Epiphany season focused on recruitment, conflict management,
evaluation, and resource assessment skills.

One parachurch group, Coalition for Christian Outreach, fo-
cuses on college students in universities across the United States
and demonstrates taking hold in another way. One of their ministries is located at Temple University in Philadelphia. A new
staff of seven young leaders anxiously awaited the completion of

their new center, Discipleship House, a base for their ministry to students. They waited with a great deal of frustration over construction delays in what I would call an Advent mode. However, to their surprise, they found that, in the absence of ministries to students, their sometimes "crazy Christian" way of preparing and eating meals or doing house chores was having an impact on the construction workers. The workmen noticed how they were different from other booze-laden campus groups, joyfully bearing witness to God's presence through the quality of their inner life and hospitality to the workers. One staff member commented, "I nearly missed how this staff demonstrated the joy, light, and peace of Christ to those in their midst. If God had answered my prayer to get the project quickly completed on my time schedule, this time of sharing his love would never have happened. We would have missed the opportunity to [influence] the workers." Theirs is a powerful Epiphany story of proclaiming good news. The close step of proclamation in the Christmas triad waltz had been taken.

In chapter 4 we will examine the extended Epiphany story of a boundary-busting Lutheran Church–Missouri Synod congregation in Mission, Kansas.

Proclaiming and Sending in Eastertide

On Easter Sunday morning worshipers are greeted with the news, "He is risen!" and respond, "He is risen indeed!" which is the appropriate affirmation for the forty-day period of Eastertide. Every ensuing Sunday worship service becomes a little Easter, as the hymn testifies: "Every day is Easter from now on!" The Easter message cannot be shut off on Monday or wilt with the passing of Easter lilies. Appearances by Jesus following his resurrection keep it alive in our memory.

Imagine that we walk with the disciples on the road to Emmaus, not fully comprehending this fantastic message—but then our eyes are opened to recognize the loving presence of Jesus in the breaking of bread at table. We imagine bringing our doubt and skepticism with Thomas to Jesus behind closed doors and are amazed at his invitation to believe by putting our hand in his side and touching the nail print of his hand. We jump for joy with the women who saw an empty tomb and first proclaimed the gospel message. We gather over breakfast with the disciples around a lakeside campfire, filling our stomachs with fresh fish. While there, we repeatedly affirm our love for Jesus. We take hold when we respond that we will indeed feed his sheep. We stand on Mount Olivet watching an ascending Jesus, recipients of his Great Commission: "Go therefore and make disciples of all nations, baptizing them in the name of the Father and of the Son and of the Holy Spirit, and teaching them to obey everything that I have commanded you. And remember, I am with you always, to the end of the age" (Matt. 28:18–20).

We have been prepared and equipped to proclaim the Easter message of life and are ready to be sent forth into service. We never really get over Easter. It continues to shape the stories of our personal and common life.

The waltz's close step of Eastertide can be associated with congregational life-giving experiences. While visiting Christ the Servant Lutheran Church in Louisville, Colorado, I heard a fascinating mission trip report from a group of adults in the congregation. The congregation's usual approach had been to send the youth off on mission trips, but the Spirit intervened, and the congregation offered the same opportunity to adults. Some of these adults had kids who had gone on mission trips, and they often felt cheated that they did not also have that opportunity. In the worship service they reported their experience of going to Greensburg, Kansas, to help with the rebuilding of a town that had nearly been totally destroyed by a devastating tornado a year earlier. The mission team, along with that of another Lutheran church, worked with a ministry that a group of Mennonites coordinated to build ten new houses at a time. They worked alongside the future owners of those houses, who had agreed that no one could move into his or her house until all ten homes were finished.

While in Greensburg, the mission group was deeply impressed by the determination of the townspeople to rebuild. Some civic leaders' suggestions after the tornado that they relocate the town or eliminate it altogether had been soundly rejected. Townspeople were determined to rebuild on the original town site, a goal that had been embraced by their children as well. These children had made stars with key inspirational words on them—words such as *hope, life, love,* and *faith*—and had posted them in vacant lots all over town.

The mission team members reported their experience as volunteers as a Pentecost-cycle story, pointing to the ways the Spirit worked miracles. But I heard their story from the standpoint of the citizens of Greensburg, who had been through a Good Friday experience. They awoke the morning after the storm to discover they were alive, rising out of the debris. They were risen. Now a year later, their motto is, "We are risen indeed!"

Any church narratives that affirm "We are risen indeed" with evidence of life are Eastertide stories. The waltz of the gospel goes on with the close step, taking hold of the gift of resurrection life. Initiatives that proclaim good news and send forth workers will produce a harvest of stories of live-giving relationships and ministries.

In chapter 5 we will examine the Eastertide story of a Lutheran church in North Omaha, Nebraska, that refused to die.

Proclaiming and Sending in Pentecost

The season of Pentecost spreads across a large portion of the calendar year—beginning from mid-May to mid-June and lasting until after Thanksgiving Day. It is by far the longest season—an extended time during which we, with the Spirit's presence and help, can proclaim the gospel, build the church, and work for justice, mercy, and peace in the world. The liturgical color for the season is green, symbolizing the growing or the greening of the church in the world. The same Spirit who launched the church in its mission on Pentecost Sunday continues to actively engage in its ongoing life and witness.

The weeks of Pentecost are sometimes referred to as "Ordinary Time"—not to devalue them but to indicate that the Spirit is active in the common and even routine rhythms of daily living and weekly worship. The Spirit offers gifts for a variety of ministries, then baptizes believers with the water of boldness to take hold and act in decisive ways. Look, for instance, at boldness personified in Acts 8–11. After the martyrdom of the deacon Stephen, the church had scattered in all directions. People lived in fear, lest Saul and his gang of thugs seek out others for the same fate. Chapter 8 reports on the deacon, Philip, preaching to the religious fringes in Samaria. Then he moves on to the Gaza road south of Jerusalem. While there, he meets a caravan of pilgrims from Ethiopia who were returning from worshiping in Jerusalem. One of them, a high government official from the queen's court, had been reading from a passage in Isaiah about a suffering servant and asks for an interpretation of the passage. He was a eunuch, a sexual minority member who had probably been turned away from the courtyard at the Temple in Jerusalem because he was "unclean." He may have wondered if the passage referred to him, because he likely experienced the same rejection and humiliation. But Philip, having been led by the Spirit to the water spring and to the eunuch, told him about the prophecy's fulfillment in Jesus. The convincing powers of the Spirit fell upon the eunuch, and he asked to be baptized— an unlikely prospect in an unlikely place in an unlikely circumstance. The Spirit, not Philip, was the real evangelist; Philip's role was simply to minister to the person with whom the Spirit was already working. (Later, in Acts 21:8–9, we find the Spirit prompting more boundary crossing, when the four daughters of Philip function as prophets, speaking the Word of God.)

In chapter 9 we see the same pattern. Saul, a persecutor of the church, was not a likely candidate for conversion. He traveled to Damascus to persecute, imprison, and kill Christians. But the Spirit confronted him on the desert road, convicted him, and blinded him. A disciple in Damascus named Ananias dreamed by the Spirit that he was directed to visit Saul, lay hands on him, and pray for his restoration of sight. At first Ananias resisted out of fear. But the Spirit gave him courage to take a risk. In this second instance, we see that the candidate was an unlikely choice. The setting was strange. The Spirit was the evangelist. And the church's role (in the person of Ananias) was to take hold by going forth to proclaim and participate in the ministry of the Spirit.

Chapter 10 tells a similar story—this time in the north by the Mediterranean coastal towns of Caesarea and Joppa. The unlikely candidate was a military man, Cornelius, a centurion in the Italian cohort—and a Gentile. The Spirit instructed him through a dream to seek out Peter and inquire about Jesus. At the same time, the Spirit offered a unique dream to Peter, in which he was instructed to eat unclean food (an image for fraternizing with Gentiles). In a miracle of timing, the messengers of Cornelius came to Peter's gate the very next morning with an invitation for him to come. Peter took a risk, for a good Jew had no business entering the house of a Gentile. But he went and then was faced with a peculiar dilemma. Cornelius asked him about Jesus, and Peter explained the best he could about the gospel of this Jesus, which was not for this Gentile! But in the middle of the explanation, the Spirit came upon Cornelius and others in his house. They asked to be baptized in the name of Jesus. Peter hesitated, but concluded that these Gentiles really believed and that he must do so, crossing a well-established boundary.

When the good folks in Jerusalem heard about it, they called Peter to come to the city and explain himself. He did so, telling this dramatic story and concluding, "Look, you guys. I was not trying to convert him. I just answered his question. God converted him! What else could I do but baptize him?" Note again that the church's role was to go forth and proclaim the gospel in response to Spirit who went before them.

In reading the whole book of the acts of the Holy Spirit through believers, along with the letters to the churches, we see a pattern that informs our response to God's calling in the long season of Pentecost. We do not need to fear boredom with the ordinary— for the extraordinary enlivens the time. We must notice where the Spirit is already at work and go there. The Pentecost season of our stories closes the third step of the waltz triad. From the standpoint of the personal journey of faith, we may ask ourselves:

Where do I experience power and energy in my life?
Where is the Spirit working beyond and within me?
In what am I confident and fulfilled?

In this ordinary time for organizations and congregations, we will want to listen to the voices on the edges in order to discern the stirrings of the Spirit in the world. Even when we have planned well for ways to take hold of mission and service initiatives, events may interrupt our plans. Much of Jesus's ministry was occasioned by interruptions. We may need to retool and take hold in new ways—to stay on our dancing toes.

On a Tuesday night in June 1980, while I moderated a deacons meeting at First Presbyterian Church in Grand Island, Nebraska, a warning came that a tornado was approaching our town. We moved to the basement, made a series of warning phone calls to members of our families, and prayed. Then several tornadoes hit. Eventually, we learned that guests from a nearby motel had been dislodged and taken to the local hospital, but they had not been admitted. So we organized to send the church van to the hospital to pick them up and bring them to the church. After that we reorganized as a hospitality center, placing a lantern at the church entrance and setting up a registration desk to track folks who came in. We also made a list of people who were missing and being searched for. Seven tornadoes ravaged our town that night, and electricity failed all over town. At 4:00 a.m. we reorganized again to send out teams to visit our own church families whose homes had been blown away. By 9:00 a.m. the Red Cross and Mennonite Disaster Relief organizations opened operations in our church building, and we began to serve meals. By late morning we reorganized again with other congregations to form an interchurch response. Over a nine-day period, twenty thousand meals were served out of the church kitchen. Over the next several days, the board of deacons repeatedly reorganized their work in response to newly discovered needs. The following Saturday they met again to place one hundred dollar bills in envelopes for delivery to fifty of our congregation's dislodged member families. One deacon asked, "Did we ever adjourn last Tuesday night's meeting?" We had not, so a motion was made to adjourn. It had been eighty-six hours long—to our knowledge the longest meeting in the history of our church—and was the result of an interruption!

The season of this story was surely Pentecost—a time to repeatedly respond with compassion to changing circumstances. Ordinary time became extraordinary kingdom-come time. The experience with the Spirit in ministry spiritually formed the deacons and congregation in the way they addressed their opportunity for ministry. Prior to the tornados, a familiar mantra in deacons meetings was, "Let us show you why that idea won't work." After the tornados it read, "With God's help, we will do it."

In chapter 6 we will look at an extended story of Pentecost life in Trinity Episcopal Church in Independence, Missouri—the "Truman Church."

WALTZING TO THE ETERNAL RHYTHMS

We have now taken nine waltz steps, three in waiting and yearning—(Advent, Lent, and pre-Pentecost), three in naming and celebrating (Christmas, Easter, and Pentecost), and three in proclaiming and sending (Epiphany, Eastertide, and the ordinary time of Pentecost). Sequentially the waltz time moves through Advent, Christmas, Epiphany; Lent, Easter, Eastertide; pre-Pentecost, Pentecost, and the ordinary time of Pentecost.

The divine rhythm we first identified in the practice of spiritual direction threaded through various spiritual practices, then surfaced in moments of the worship hours and wound its way through the days of Holy Week. In this chapter, we have seen that rhythm in the weeks of the church year. We are now ready to look more closely at several important stories from churches named Trinity, connect them to church seasons, and mine them for wisdom.

CHAPTER 4

The Christmas Triad in Churches Named Trinity

JULIET:
'Tis but thy name that is my enemy;
Thou art thyself, though not a Montague

O, be some other name!
What's in a name? that which we call a rose
By any other name would smell as sweet;
So Romeo would, were he not Romeo call'd,
Retain that dear perfection which he owes
Without that title. Romeo, doff thy name,
And for that name which is no part of thee
Take all myself.

—WILLIAM SHAKESPEARE,
ROMEO AND JULIET, ACT 2, SCENE 2

When Juliet suggests that a rose by any other name would be just as sweet, she dismisses the formative power of one's name. She urges Romeo to claim his own personal identity and charism, or special gift, rather than be dominated by the name Montague—to jettison his name, for it is no part of him. I take exception. My experience confirms a theme found in storytelling through the ages that people and institutions become their names and live them out in daily activities. I have seen it in my own family. Two of our sons are each named for a different grandfather and have taken on subtle characteristics from each respective side of the family.

Can it also be true that congregations become their names? Does Christ the Servant Church live out its own life any differently than Christ the King Church? Does being a "first church" create subtle or not so subtle attitudes and postures? Does the name Independent Presbyterian Church create a confusion of identity and authority, given the fact that the very essence of Presbyterianism is connectional? Do churches that bear the names of saints or biblical characters take on their charisms? What about Trinity churches? Will they function any differently from churches with a different name, even though both affirm a trinitarian theology and spirituality? I think they will tend to interpret their stories more often in that light. But that remains an open question for us to consider as we move through this book.

In seeking congregational stories that connect with the seasons of the church year and name God's presence as a loving God, suffering but risen servant, and empowering Spirit, I am drawn to churches named Trinity. I want to see if and how they live out their name. In this chapter and the two that follow, I tell their stories. I invite readers to think about whether congregations named Trinity are any different from others, based on the stories presented here and other congregations of which the readers are aware. What do you think?

TO LOVE IS TO REMEMBER
An Advent Story from Holy Trinity Orthodox Church, Overland Park, Kansas

"The gift of memory, as the power that transforms love into life, knowledge, communion, and unity, has been given to man by God. Man's memory is his responding love for God, encounter and communion with God, and with the life of life itself. Out of all creation it is given to man alone to remember God and through this remembrance to truly live."[1]

Holy Trinity Orthodox Church was birthed in 1917 by Russian immigrants in a neighborhood known as Russian Hill in Kansas City, Kansas. The cornerstone of the original church, which was constructed that same year, identifies it as "Russian Greek Orthodox Church." Today the relocated church in Overland Park, Kansas, is related to the Diocese of the Midwest of the Orthodox Church in America. Over the past nine decades Holy Trinity Orthodox Church has grown from a small Russian-speaking parish to one whose two hundred members are primarily American-born, English-speaking converts to Orthodoxy. They identify themselves as "a growing church community worshiping God—Father, Son, and Holy Spirit—in the 2000-year-old Orthodox Christian Tradition."

The story of how this small, struggling, ethnic neighborhood church became a vital faith community could be placed in any season of the church year. The congregation lives out a strong trinitarian consciousness in worship, spiritual formation, and outreach. Their central worship experience of the Pascha, the feast of the resurrection, could place them at Easter. Their attention to the Holy Spirit in liturgy and life could locate their story at Pentecost. But the real story of their emergence and transformation locates them in the Advent-Christmas cycle. They traversed a long Advent-like journey of waiting, hoping, and yearning that began in 1978 with the assignment of a young priest and culminated some twenty-four years later with the celebration of the Pascha in a new beautiful and spacious worship space, what they call a "temple."

When Father John Platko came to Holy Trinity in 1978, he found a small, dispirited band of mostly second and some third generation worshipers. Their immigrant forbearers had settled in the United States on a hill overlooking the Kansas and Missouri rivers, stockyards, and meat packing plants of Kansas City, where many found employment. The congregation had made the transition from Slavonic to English-speaking worship services. They had shifted from an immigrant consciousness to that of being American, but with declining numbers, they were not able to support a full-time priest for an extended period of time. Their clergy leadership became sporadic. One member remarked, "If we had fifteen people in church, that was a big crowd!" In the 1970s they feared that they would be shut down by the bishop.

Father Platko's role in this Advent-like story could be likened to that of John the Baptist. He announced in word and deed, "Prepare the way of the Lord." He brought an unusual set of talents to this new church. He sang the liturgy with a beautiful, strong voice. He wrote and arranged music. He knew how to relate to young people. His congenial temperament endeared him to the few remaining members, who were willing to work together with him for the good of the church.

He was a master carpenter who inherited a deteriorating building that was hard to heat in winter months and had a badly leaking roof. He addressed the immediate need to renovate the building—mostly through volunteer labor and members' contributions. Shortly after he arrived the congregation committed itself to repair the building at an estimated cost of fifty thousand dollars. The roof was repaired, bricks repointed, windows replaced, twenty-nine outside steps replaced, cupola rebuilt, interior renovated, inside staircase finished, choir loft propped up, a balcony added, the altar beautified, and new icons added.

The close-knit group of members worked hard. They raised money via the festivals in their neighborhood of Strawberry Hill, sometimes called Russian Hill. They toiled as volunteers, refusing to go into debt as a matter of principle, although they did benefit from the interest earnings of a trust that had been left by a deceased member. The council had voted that the interest from the trust could not be used for general expenses. That decision provided a boost to accomplish these special projects for the "church on the hill."

After completing the renovation, the congregation experienced some growth, and they intended to remain in that location. But they were becoming more of a regional church and less a neighborhood church to which members could walk. Their strong family-oriented life both held them together and gave them the capacity to welcome visitors to church. Younger visitors were often embraced and adopted as though they were part of members' families.

But Father Platko's leadership role for this church in its Advent season extended far beyond refurbishing a building. Their successful renovation proved that they had capabilities that extended beyond surviving on the hill. This accomplishment became a sign, giving them courage to look ahead and dream a larger future. Most of their third generation members had moved to the suburban fringes of Kansas City but continued to commute to Strawberry Hill for worship. They needed to expand their facilities to hold their existing members and incorporate new growth. To complicate matters, however, the city would not allow additional expansion on the hill and they were severely limited in parking. Some of the wise second generation members concluded that they would need to relocate if they hoped to survive and eventually grow. In the mid-1980s, shortly after the renovations were completed, Father John offered a vision for a new, larger temple in a new location. "Have faith," he said. "Keep praying. We will grow, and God will make it happen." He shifted the focus to a vision of the far distant future. But at the same time, he did not discount the rich heritage of faith that preceded this Advent story.

They celebrated their history and life together in a commemorative book, *To Love Is to Remember*. It drew on the insights of a 1975 article by an Orthodox priest, Father Alexander Schmemann, on the subject of memory. They affirmed, "The future of our Church depends on us, not just on our strength and ability, but above all on our obedience to Christ and to the wonderful heritage He has bestowed on us. . . . A common past, a common destiny is made up not only of victories and achievements but also of failure and defeats experienced together and understood in the light of God's will."[2] Throughout this period of waiting and yearning, leaders gave special attention to those who bore the memories of the old days by listening to their stories and viewing old pictures.

The church continued to wait, hope, work, and learn. When they realized they could not expand on their current site, they began to look around for a new church site, but with no particular destination in mind. Then by happenstance they learned about a six-acre farm that had become available about ten miles to the south in Johnson County, Kansas, at the corner of 119th Street and Pflumm Road. Some said the property came to them as a fluke. Others point to Divine Providence. The sellers were an older couple who wanted their dairy farm with its old house to go to a church.

In 1993 the congregation voted by a 75 percent majority to purchase the six acres for eighty-three thousand dollars. For many the day contained a mixture of both sadness and joy. Their decision pointed them in a new direction, although at the time they could not have pictured the thousands of cars that would pass this busy corner every day. While taking the vote, most members were sensitive to the older second generation who still lived in the neighborhood on the hill. But one recognized sage, John Super, counseled his contemporaries that this was the correct course to take if they wanted to grow. Everyone in the church knew him, loved him, and called him Uncle John. He had been a mainstay in maintaining the property and spirit of the community on the hill. Now his counsel helped sway his generation of members and offered a blessing to the next generation. The decision could not have been made without a prayerful posture of relinquishment and letting go of a meaningful association with a historic location.

The time seemed right, a characteristic of the Advent season. We are reminded that God sent his Son into the world in "the fullness of time" (Gal. 4:4). That historic era of peace, open Roman roads, and the Diaspora of Jews throughout the Mediterranean world opened the doors for the expansion of the Christian religion in the world. Now this congregation was aware that their waiting and yearning would culminate in a new day—one God was preparing for them. The decision had come in God's own time. An inner voice of God seemed to say, "Do it now." They did it.

For eight years after the decision to purchase the farm site, the church continued to operate on the hill but took steps to adopt the new property. They did not erect a sign on the property, but the farm became a prime location for picnics and outings. The old house was fixed up for the congregation's temporary use. At times the community would worship on Strawberry Hill, then go to a party at the farm to listen to the Kansas City Chiefs football games. Vacation church school for children was held at the farm.

The new site became an alternative location for fund-raising events. Bake sales were held. Tomatoes and pumpkins were raised and sold from a garden members had cultivated. The church leaders wanted to make the transition a gradual one that would increase the comfort level for all. During one of the bake sales the family whose parents had sold their farm to the church came by to visit. Their visit became a blessing to both the selling family and the soon to be relocated church. The land bound them together in the fulfillment of a common destiny.

A crucial third decision in the congregation's life was whether to actually build a new temple on the farm site. The specially called congregational meeting drew one hundred of the one hundred twenty members, the highest attendance the church had ever had for a deliberative meeting. This vote would offer the final test of their intention to follow the leading of the Holy Spirit. Much was at stake, not only for the older members who were faced with the losses of a neighborhood church on the hill, the convenience of walking to church, and a tangible reminder for their stories but also for third generation members who had come to love their adopted holy place with its view overlooking downtown Kansas

City. The old building had been valued as a warm, secure place. It had been an attractive beacon on a hill. What would their church be in the new setting—a flat, open farm field?

A small band of people, most of whom were not independently wealthy, were faced with a seven-figure price tag for a new temple. The decision was a hard, heart-wrenching one, but the final vote was 98 percent in favor of the decision to move and build. One participant described it as an unforgettable and humbling church experience. He observed elderly people unselfishly voting in favor, simply because it seemed to be the right thing to do. Over the eight years, they had moved from a 75 percent vote to buy the farm to a 98 percent approval to actually build and relocate there—a testimony to their determination to follow God's leading.

A prompt sale of the old church meant that they would have to move into temporary space before going into the new church. The old church had never been consecrated; therefore it could still be used for other purposes and its value was enhanced for potential buyers. It was sold to an artist in the community who intended to use it for a video production business and also to live in the lower level.

The closing of the church on Russian Hill took place July 8, 2001. The service was conducted with the same patient care as the plans for the new church. A video that included pictures and stories from 1917 to 2001 was prepared and shown near the time of the closing. The second generation members recorded stories of their memories, difficulties, hopes, and joys on audiotape for use by future generations. The blessings offered by this group freed the next generation from any guilt that they had "fled to the suburbs of Johnson County."

The final Pascha celebrated in the old church (in 2001) was memorable, for the announcement that "Christ is risen" was heard for the last time at midnight in that darkened and candlelit space. Tears arose from both joy and sadness, but worshipers were touched by Christ's triumph over the grave. The next day the congregation gathered to celebrate the Agape Feast. The children, now the fourth generation of members, were taken up past the choir loft onto a series of steps that led to the bell tower. They had never visited it before. From that location in the "louvers room," they looked over the city, took pictures, and rang the bell. The bell, located in the cupola atop the tower, was to be removed and re-hung in the tower of the new temple. One adult supervisor of the visit called it "one of the coolest memories of my life."

Many group pictures were taken on that last day, and Father John planned the dismantling of artifacts and furnishings and made arrangements for their care during the interim days. These items were to be kept in the homes of the church members, who would make them available for weekly worship and when special feast days called for them. At that last service on the hill, the icon of the Ascension was taken down and rolled up for storage in one member's basement. When it was eventually reinstalled in the new church, it was in perfect condition.

People claimed their role as stewards of the worship accents with honor and respect. For the next nine months, the congregation would worship in a middle school near the new site. In that space they would need liturgical furnishings, the baptismal font, and holy water for weekly worship and for special festivals, such as the celebration of Theophany, a time of baptismal renewal coinciding with the celebration of Jesus's baptism and the beginning of the season of Epiphany. Members' personal stewardship of the items became an important spiritual discipline for them. They needed to make items available in order to claim the temporary worship environment as holy space for their use. One member reminisced: "We were meeting in the cafeteria of the school surrounded by cartoon characters painted on the walls. Then we moved upstairs into the gym for worship and had to cover up the school's mascot that was painted on the wall above where the altar would be. Everything had to be carried in, set up and taken down—altar, icons, service books, and coffee hour items."[3]

During those months of worshiping in the middle school, and then when the congregation began to worship in the new church, the younger members showed their care for the older members by going to the hill to pick them up and bring them to worship.

Worshiping near the new church site, members' waiting and yearning became more and more intense. They watched over every small detail of the emerging structure. They smiled when they learned that the old church bell would not fit through the openings in the new cupola, so the bell had to be installed before the roof was put on. Parishioners exclaimed, "It is never coming out of there!" The chandelier from the old church was hung to grace the narthex. Folks watched closely as the icons were put in place. *The Hospitality of Abraham,* a manifestation of the Trinity, was hung on the left panel of the icon screen, which in Orthodox churches is placed between the sanctuary, where the Eucharist is celebrated, and the nave, where the congregation stands or sits. The icon *The Epiphany of Our Lord* was hung on the right side. Both icons prayerfully affirm the Trinity, which is central not only to the congregation's name but also for its identity and ethos. The icons offer a prayerful entrance into reflection upon their experiences in light of God's threefold presence.

An open house was scheduled so that people in the community could come inside and look at this new Byzantine-style building. It is traditional, yet modern. Visitors testified that it really looked like a beautiful church, not like some other churches in the region!

The most difficult aspect at this point in the congregation's Advent story was the need to take out a mortgage. The new building cost 1.3 million dollars and was not paid for, and the mortgage was the congregation's first experience with indebtedness. Their treasurer said, "We were a little band of parishioners with a monster mortgage." But even the mortgage became part of their walk of faith. The Christmas carol reminded them that "the hopes and fears of all the years" were part of the Advent story.

In Holy Week of 2002, the folks who had yearned, worked, and waited for nine long years entered the sacred space of their beautiful, spacious new temple for worship. The narthex alone measured thirty-by-thirty feet, larger than their nave had been in the old church, where people had stood around the edges for special services. Now they all could be seated. Entering the new space became an incredible experience for these people. One recalled the Pascha that year: "At the midnight service, when all of the lights are extinguished except for a single candle on the altar, the sound of strong male voices accompanies the passing of light to illuminate a packed church. It feels like a new beginning and an icon of the world."[4] Years of anticipation heightened their experience. One person who returned to the sanctuary forty-five minutes after the service had ended observed the smell and haze of the incense that had been burned and was deeply aware that "Something had happened. God had acted. We were anointed." It was a new beginning, indeed—doubly celebrated the next morning when people gathered again over food to celebrate Christ's resurrection.

The events of that Holy Week and Easter tied the bow on the Christmas present of this Advent story. God had indeed loved them so much that God gave them a gift. Uncle John Super played a role somewhat similar to that of Simeon, the old man in the temple who exclaimed, "Now you are dismissing your servant in peace . . . for my eyes have seen your salvation" (Luke 2:29, 30). Years before Uncle John had predicted, "The church will move after we are gone." He now says, "I never thought I would live to see the day. I never thought we would get to this point." But he did live to see the day—and though confined to a nursing home, he continues to praise God for the unfolding story of love and grace.

If we were to extend this story into Epiphany, we would see the light of Christ extending into the world around Holy Trinity. The congregation did not experience explosive growth, as many megachurches do, but a steady growth that went deep. They are a congregation of Smiths, Joneses, and Johnsons as well as Ethiopians, Serbians, Russians, and Greeks. They currently attract young seekers from mainline Protestant denominations. One new young convert describes her transition: "As a little girl I only associated Easter with pretty little new dresses. But when I experienced the sadness and mourning of Holy Week, the rejoicing of Pascha, the empty tomb, the community celebration of the Agape Feast, I felt at home. This was the place for me." T h e church tends to hold special attraction for young families. When asked why, one young parent responded, "Because of the church's flexibility, longevity, authenticity, trinitarian orientation, consecration of all life, and inclusion of children in every aspect of life and worship."

An icon, *The Pantokrator* (Christ, the Almighty and Ruler of All), was installed at the top of the dome over the nave in 2007. After it was installed, the scaffolding was left up so that people could go up for a closer look at the icon. One mother recalled, "As my eighteen-month-old daughter kissed the icon of Christ after climbing with me up the scaffolding, I whispered in her ear, 'When you get married in this church, look up and you will know!'"

A postscript to the story must be added. Their beloved Father John Platko was diagnosed with pancreatic cancer shortly after they moved into the new temple. He died in 2005 after serving the church for twenty-six years. His welcoming spirit lives in the icon of *Jesus' Blessing of the Children,* which was installed in the narthex in 2007 as a memorial to him. There, lighted by the chandelier from the old church, it offers a welcome consistent with his spirit.

But he did not leave the church leaderless. Before his death, he had invited Father Timothy Sawchak to assist him and to succeed him as priest to Holy Trinity. Father Tim had worshiped with the church while attending the University of Kansas as an architectural student in 1983, so he was intimately acquainted with the long and rich story of the church. Uncle John said of him, "He came at the right time."

THEY RETURNED BY ANOTHER WAY
An Epiphany Story from
Trinity Lutheran Church, Mission, Kansas

Trinity Lutheran Church of Mission, Kansas, a Johnson County suburb of the greater Kansas City metropolitan area, has gained the reputation for and adopted a self-image of pushing and busting boundaries.[5] Their current mission statement proudly proclaims, "We are relentless in knowing Christ and fearless in making him known." This attitude is nothing new to them, for they have operated this way since the Lutheran Church—Missouri Synod (LCMS) congregation was founded in the late 1940s. Pushing and busting boundaries is their spiritual DNA.

Their founding pastor, Harlan Hartner, brought a knack for friendship, a capacity to share the gospel, and a commitment to involvement in the community. Pastor Roland Boehnke, who followed Hartner, continued to expose the congregation to contemporary strategies for church development, renewal, and outreach. The pastors and congregation were not shy about trying new things. The congregation absorbed Boehnke's venturesome spirit.

Lee Hovel, the current senior pastor, originally came to the congregation as an associate pastor who had been connected with Concordia Seminary in Exile (often referred to as "Seminex"), a progressive LCMS seminary. It was formed after a walkout by a group of students and faculty at Concordia Seminary in St. Louis, the denomination's largest seminary, in a conservative-liberal tug-of-war that came to a head in 1974. Pastor Hovel's leadership of Trinity Lutheran Church favors the Epiphany season. That should not be surprising, given the congregation's propensity for "coming back by another way," as the magi did after their encounter with the holy family.

Celebrations at Christmas draw this congregation into a keen awareness of a loving and giving God. Three trees grace the

sanctuary, all joined to a star connected to the trees by stream-
ers. Stars, moon, and sun decorate one tree in testimony of the
creative power of God. Crowns of thorns decorate the second tree
in tribute to the Son, who gave his life for the salvation of the
world. Doves and seashells decorate the third tree as evidence of
the power of the Holy Spirit, who draws people into discipleship
through the waters of baptism. People who enter Trinity Lutheran
Church at Christmas will be welcomed by the Bethlehem creche
located in the large narthex, will observe three windows and three
pillars in the sanctuary, and finally will focus on the three trees.
They cannot avoid noticing the symbolism and commitment to
and expression of trinitarian faith.

When worshipers hear the story of the magi at Christmas and
beyond, they know boundaries have been broken. God's gift tran-
scends provincialism. Even as the magi returned by another route
(Matt. 2:12), this church invites its worshipers to explore paths
for worship, witness, and service never before traversed. They
emphasize mission and outreach immediately after celebrating
Christmas. That period is not observed as ordinary dead time to
get ready for Lent and Easter. On the Sunday following the day of
Epiphany, they are invited to remember their own baptism as they
consider the baptism of Jesus. Baptism begins the journey into
discipleship. It is a time to take hold and care about the world Jesus came to redeem—and to care while taking new paths. All who
have been baptized during the previous year bring a candle as a
remembrance, renewing their baptism together with all who have
been baptized in the years before.

The Epiphany season ends at the Mount of Transfiguration.
At both Jesus's baptism and transfiguration, God's voice boomed,
"This is my beloved Son." Jesus's Galilean ministry between these
two declarations broke through old boundaries to embrace a gospel that would include all people in every circumstance. While
picking up fishing nets to become fishers for people, the folks at
Trinity consider their calling to participate in restoring the world

to God's original intention. They prepare to discover new paths for witness and service.

With a strong trinitarian orientation and inclination to Epiphany outreach, this congregation evidences its DNA to be boundary busters with a risky passion for mission. They were the first church in the Kansas District to employ a director of Christian education as a youth pastor. Positioned near the first high school in the area, Trinity drew students to its new after-school programs. They were the first congregation in Johnson County to open a preschool—one that still exists. They were first to employ a minister of gifts—even before that theme became popular. They seeded the development of six new congregations with delegations from their own membership and start-up funds. Their church choir performed at Carnegie Hall in New York City.

Their church council participated in a developmental model to integrate spirituality and administration through an ecumenical project conducted by Worshipful-Work. I had an opportunity to work with them in developing the model. They created agendas for their meetings that matched the worship structure of their Sunday morning services. A recent congregational meeting was designed around a rhythm of worship with participants pausing for prayer three times.

Trinity was a charter member of Metropolitan Lutheran Ministries (MLM), a program that adopts families and provides furniture and job skills for the poor. MLM found housing for more than four hundred families. Trinity raised $187,000 through a neighborhood garage sale to support the MLM mission. When Trinity church looks at its own life and outreach, they see a model of relationships—both among themselves and with the surrounding world. As a result, more than a tithe of the congregation's income is committed to mission and outreach.

The members represent a wide spectrum of learning styles, thus calling for a wide diversity of worship expressions from contemporary to traditional to contemplative—more boundary busting. Contemporary services use screens, visual images, drama, and a variety of music. A contemporary service was started twenty years ago at a time when this style of worship was not particularly in vogue. In their commitment to inclusiveness, women and men serve together at the communion table, and women have been invited to deliver sermons from the pulpit— not a common practice in the LCMS.

The congregation's boundary-busting attitude even resulted in changing the walls of the church building. The original church, constructed in the 1940s, was built with the entrance positioned at the eastern point of a pie-shaped lot. But as additional parking was made available, most folks used a different entrance, walking down narrow hallways through doors that funneled them near the chancel area and into the nave, often drawing attention away from those leading the service. So they radically redesigned the church, turning it 180 degrees, and created out of a combination of small rooms and hallways an attractive, open welcoming space for people as they entered from the parking lot. Now those who enter the worship space come in from the back of the sanctuary and, to their surprise, are able to see the beautiful stained glass window at the front (formerly the back) and no longer hidden by a balcony. Trinitarian substance has not changed. But style has.

In the late 1980s an electronic media board was constructed, at some considerable cost, at the point of the lot, tastefully positioned into the landscape where it was dramatically visible for passersby who traversed a busy parkway—a first for churches in the area. It was so effective that some travelers complained that the potential distractions could create a safety hazard.

Their attempt in 2008–2009 at church extension (the seventh) follows another relatively untried path—operating one church on two campuses with one budget, a unified board, and shared staff. Whereas they had previously used a familiar church-planting model, they determined this time to proceed by a different route.

New research shows that 80 percent of new church starts fail if the new church plant is only sent people and money from a mother church. New congregations want and deserve autonomy and freedom to earn their own way, thereby enhancing their own commitment to grow and develop. Trinity's leaders recognized that strategies for planting new congregations had changed. And the congregation had changed. The East Campus on the original site has five hundred members over age fifty-five and one hundred members over age eighty. People in the neighborhood are growing older, with fewer children living in close proximity. Houses that turn over are not attracting families with children but attract singles who share homes and other older people who want to live closer to the center of the city.

Meanwhile the West campus, located eleven miles to the west in Johnson County, a major growth edge to the southwest of the Kansas City metropolitan area, is made up of members in their thirties with children. The church recognizes that both centers need each other for mutual mentoring and outreach. Yet they also experience the struggle and tension inherent in experimenting with multisite ministry. For some, sharing a pastor is just not the same as having one dedicated to a particular site. Not all decisions of the council meet with unanimous approval, and leaders of the staff and council may seem more distant, with resulting signs of suspicion or resistance among members.

So the barrier-breaking culture for which the congregation has been known over the years is being tested. The tailwinds of change that have supported the Epiphany-like movements outward have slowed. The double-campus configuration threatens the established routines at one location and the resulting comfort level that had developed over the years. Have they fallen victim to an organization life cycle that tests the congregation's radical self-image? Gentrification and stagnation offer headwinds for this congregation with a historic bent to creativity. Two examples expose the issues.

The oldest preschool in Johnson County, which originated on the East Campus, was moved to the West Campus. The West Campus was using a revamped office building for its gatherings, and an adjacent building was also available for their use. Moving the preschool was feasible and placed the school in proximity to many more children and the younger families in the church. But the sounds of children and the additional traffic that the school brought to the East Campus were missed. Headwinds arose. The old campus was not the same anymore.

Scheduling worship, given the pressing needs for adult Bible study on Sunday mornings, presented a second headwind. Two task forces, one from each campus, were asked to explore and recommend a design and schedule for Sunday morning worship. Both recommended moving to two services on each campus and blending the contemporary practices of the East campus into both services on both campuses. The recommendations met resistance, particularly from active participants in the middle contemporary service on the East campus who feared their service would be taken away. A special, well-attended, and prayerful congregational meeting was called, and a resolution was adopted to maintain the contemporary service as it was, although over the years it had transitioned from contemporary to gospel-country.

How could the congregation's avowed cultural aim to take risks in all aspects of its life and mission, to live out its "relentless" and "fearless" character, now express itself in light of the resistance that arose after moving the preschool and proposing changes in worship? That became the question for the council to discern.

The leaders looked again to their own roots and were led to call the congregation to a conscious identity of servant leadership. The council identified itself as a "Board of Servant Leaders." Servanthood would become the focus for study groups and worship services during the season of Lent in 2009.

Could this identity for ministry catch on for individuals, small mission groups, and the congregation at large? Some began to grasp the notion of leading by serving. One member described her activities across the years in the church as very church centered with energy expended in raising her family, supporting women's activities, and sharing fellowship that grew out of study classes. Now she finds herself in the West Campus with a new challenge and opportunity to engage in outreach. She prays, "God, I want you to use me. Show me what you want me to do to make this campus succeed!" She assumes a personal ministry of outreach, helping people enter the doors, inviting them to return, and helping them connect to small groups, study classes, and any activities that would prevent them from entering the dropout track. "For me, it is a change and it is more than a life stage that I am going through. I am genuinely passionate about it!"

To ensure that servanthood takes root for the whole congregation and for isolated individuals, the church council recently made another barrier-busting decision. On the first Sunday after Easter they were to dispense with all structured worship services in order to free their members to engage in volunteer service initiatives in the community on that day. One member says, "It is not viewed as a day off from church." Over thirty servant opportunities were planned that extended into the city. They were to incorporate direct personal service—working on a Habitat for Humanity house, cleaning for people, and helping out in various ways—and create new relationships with individuals and groups with specific needs. Special service opportunities for people with physical limitations were to be set up in homes and in church buildings. This special service day has potential to be a catalyst for future servant-oriented activities. Momentum was building, and only time and the Spirit will tell whether it will propel the congregation into new arenas for barrier busting.

So how does Trinity church live out its name? Pastor Hovel cites the explanation of the Trinity in Martin Luther's Small Catechism.

In the first article, Creation, God the Father creates, supports and protects body and soul. Therefore, we are thankful. In the second article, Redemption, Jesus, God's Son, redeems and sets us free.

In the third article, Sanctification, the Holy Spirit calls, gathers, sanctifies, and enlightens us. So, when we confess the creed, we engage in the practice of telling God's story. And we are telling our own story as well—within our own spiritual DNA. We take God's story and our story to the world, where we practice and tell an ongoing story.

This Trinitarian identity, which goes farther and deeper than all the threefold symbols in the entryway and sanctuary, propels our members to live out the congregation's motto, "Relentless in knowing Christ and fearless in making him known."[6]

This affirmation of faith and purpose statement will be enacted over and over again with a congregation that sees itself as an Epiphany church, choosing to return by another way after they have encountered and celebrated the love of God in Christmas.

CHAPTER 5

The Easter Triad
in Churches Named Trinity

While looking at the stories of churches that have contemplated the possibility of closing their doors and ending life as they have known it, I am struck with how many of their stories fit into the season of Lent, Holy Week, and Easter. These congregations face the possibility of death head on—with the accompanying dynamics of fear, mistrust, denial, betrayal, guilt, posturing, and hope. Just as Jesus set his face toward Jerusalem (Luke 9:51) and spoke openly with his disciples about his impending death, these churches pull back the curtain of silence and denial to consider the possibility of dying with dignity, closing with compassion, ending with strength, and sometimes even transitioning into new life.

THEY RAISED THREE BELLS
Holy Trinity Church, Centerville, Montana

When Father Thomas Murphy became bishop of the Roman Catholic Diocese of Great Falls-Billings in Montana, he inherited a number of small, struggling, mission outposts that had been created across the years to serve outlying communities of miners, farmers, and ranchers. He saw the need to close these missions but did not want to impose a decision upon them that would destroy their spirit. He invited several sisters from the Sisters of Charity of the Blessed Virgin Mary, whose motherhouse was located in Dubuque, Iowa, to come to the diocese and serve as pastoral administrators of small parishes. He also assigned them to lead several of the struggling missions in order to help those churches explore their future, which could include the option of closing. If they were to close, Bishop Murphy wanted them to end with hope.

Sister Deanna Carr was assigned to three outposts near Great Falls: the missions of St. Francis Xavier in Eden and St. Paul in Sand Coulee, and Saints Cyril and Methodius Church at Stockett. The church and missions had originally been established to serve Eastern Europeans who had come to Montana to work in the mines. But those mines were long since gone, and now the area was impoverished, with the remaining population trying to eke out an existence from small farms and a few livestock. Their churches were surely walking the valley of the shadow of death.

Sister Deanna patiently began to initiate conversations about the future of the missions and parish at a number of levels, both informal and formal. She created an environment where people could talk freely without being judged. People did have creative ideas. She allowed those ideas to surface as members attempted to move toward consensus. She wanted them to own the decision they would eventually make by collaborative sharing and thinking rather than by reacting to an imposed edict from the outside.

Parishioners realized that closing a church would call for a great deal of letting go. They were deeply attached to their building and its contents, for which they had given and worked across the years. Father Ted Szudera, who currently serves as priest to Holy Trinity parish, has listened to people converse about those former days of hard decision making. He says that they organize their stories around one word that always comes up—*sacrifice*. They knew the names of people who had given the pews, altar rails, statues, and specific fixtures. A favorite uncle may have created a handiwork that was important to all.

So how did these three faith communities come to eventually give up their preciously held identities and investments of time and money they had each made over the years? Sister Deanna points to three factors: (1) The people were down to earth and practical in nature. They did not try to put on airs to impress each other or the other churches. They were plainspoken folks who could discern the obvious, given their declining numbers. (2) The diocese had a shortage of priests, and the people's needs were not adequately being met. (3) The process of considering their future was greatly enhanced by the presence of a retired priest, Father Martin Werner. Whereas Sister Deanna, who led the conversations, was considered an outsider, Father Werner was the consummate insider, and the bishop had requested that he sit in on the deliberations. Everyone knew him and loved him. He employed a charming sense of humor, which became a real gift when matters became tense. He blessed their explorations and eventual conclusions.

Many informal conversations took place in local settings. And formal conversations took place with Father Werner and Sister Deanna present in a newly organized parish council, which offered a gracious space where people from all three communities could struggle together. They were able to tell and recite their unique stories. Issues common to all three communities were exchanged and considered at that table. Any eventual outcome and future relationship would need to be based on a deepening trust. Father Ted reports that years after the birth of the new parish, strong and effective pastoral parish council and finance council systems continue to function—legacies of those days of working together in trust building through the bonds of faith, hope, and love.

Facing the closure of three historic churches led them down a difficult path with Good Friday-type dynamics. But the council and three faith communities also came to rest in an Easter hope. They generated new visions for a common future. They decided to close all three churches and to establish a single new parish in Centerville, directly across from a school.

The new parish needed a name, and they discerned that as well. It would be Holy Trinity Parish in Centerville. Selecting Trinity as a name seemed obvious due to the fact that the people were drawn from three worship points. But the significance of the name Trinity surfaced from a well of deep spiritual water. While telling their stories, they affirmed that they were founded by a loving, creating God. They had been fed and nurtured across the years by the grace of Christ, and they yearned for a new common life empowered by the Spirit.

Although after the new parish was created, they met in a gymnasium for Sunday worship, the heart of their spiritual life centered in the eucharistic chapel, which housed the tabernacle of the Blessed Sacrament and was the locus for daily prayer. That chapel also housed the icon around which their life centered—the icon of the Trinity. That icon presents Abraham welcoming the strangers, a familiar story to Roman Catholic adherents.

The most visible demonstration of the three parishes' deaths and their resurrection as Holy Trinity Parish occurred when they took the three church bells from the former missions, assembled them in a tower, and raised them together. The three bells could have been melted and recast into one new bell, but each bell was allowed to peal its distinct tone and contribute to a miraculously harmonious blend. Trinity resonates through the new church.

AND THEN THEY BURIED THE ALTAR
The Roman Catholic Mission, Reed Point, Montana

Bishop Murphy brought a second sister to Montana to serve as a pastoral administrator and work with small missions. Sister Ellen Morseth, BVM, was assigned to St. Joseph parish in Big Timber and a mission outpost at Reed Point. I became acquainted with her Montana work when we worked together in training events on communal discernment called "Schools for Discernmentarians," cosponsored by Worshipful-Work and Upper Room Ministries. In those leadership events, we searched for case studies from churches through which we could probe ten identifiable movements in spiritual discernment. One of those movements invited decision makers into a prayerful mode of relinquishment, or of letting go. We asked them to identify what needed to die in them in order to make room for any growth God might offer.

Over time, we often utilized a case story Ellen brought from her experience as the pastoral administrator at Reed Point. The story was so profound and gripping that it regularly became a show stopper for our training groups. People sat in silent awe. Her story centered on the practice of using the lectionary readings in the seasons of the church year as an aid to making important and difficult decisions. Her story gathered steam in Lent and exploded in Holy Week. The story became a mainstay case study that we repeatedly examined in each group with which we worked.

Ellen's story was talked about in a number of circles and eventually came to the attention of Beth Gaede, who was editing a new book on church closings, *Ending with Hope*, for the Alban Institute. The book contains contributions from fifteen authors who cite specific dynamics, stories, and resources from fifteen congregations and a wealth of material from lay, pastoral, judicatory, and seminary leaders. Ellen's story was placed in chapter 1 to lead the parade. The book is about Easter, but the struggles and searching that most congregations went through is very Lenten. Here is Sister Ellen's Lenten story from *Ending with Hope*.

I was invited by a bishop to assume responsibility as pastoral administrator (a lay person or deacon appointed by a bishop to pastor and administer a parish) of a parish in Montana and its mission church, 35 miles due east. During the course of our conversations, I remember the bishop telling me that the mission church "should have been closed a number of years ago, but no previous pastor had the nerve to do it." Then he told me that he would like me to accomplish this task!

As someone who did not relish being a new pastoral presence with such a goal in mind, I asked the bishop to give me at least three years to assess the situation and to accomplish in some collaborative way an outcome that would be the best decision for everyone involved. Thankfully, he agreed. Then the thought of figuring out how to facilitate significant, prayerful conversations about the life of this long-standing mission church gave me much food for thought and prayer.

My first undertaking over many months was to get to know the people and to be a helpful pastoral presence in their midst. Every Saturday I led their worship service, and before and after the service I engaged in social conversation with whoever was there. Though I intentionally resisted jumping to conclusions about the life of this small congregation, it did not take me long to observe many disturbing facets of their life. For example, the church once having 35 members now had a roster of 12, three to six of whom participated regularly in weekly services. The average weekly stewardship collection was $3.00. And the building, a simple wood structure with no plumbing, desperately needed a new roof. Then, too, I learned that the adults wanted me to provide religious education classes for their children in their town one evening a week, rather than the parents taking some responsibility for bringing their children to already organized classes at the mother church. These parishioners also seemed to think their participation in adult education events and retreats was totally out of the question.

My overall discovery was that for the majority of parishioners, "church" meant a building of convenience. And my ministry was taken for granted. This small community seemed unwilling—and in some cases the people were just not able— to take responsibility for their own religious growth, for stewardship of the building and land, and for a relationship with the larger diocesan faith community.

After one year as their minister, my attempts to initiate conversations about ongoing formation for ministry, stewardship, and a relationship to the larger diocese seemed to have fallen on deaf ears. This congregation's life appeared to be stuck in neutral gear, and I was becoming more convinced that some decision about its life had to be made—and owned—by the people involved. But I had no positive case studies to guide me on the ways of closing or merging Catholic parishes.

After much thought and prayer about this situation, I became inspired to use the three-year cycle of Sunday lectionary readings as a focus for spiritual discernment via communal storytelling and reflection on the life of this mission church. This took place from 1985 to 1987—literally evolving week by week—without a strategic plan. I invited stories about the history of the small town and how the church came to be. We looked at the data from old newspapers collected in the diocesan archives, and one of the "old-timers" shared some photographs from horse and buggy days. The parishioners talked about the good times as well as their families' lives during the [D]epression. Through all the storytelling, I was trying to help all of us see the big picture up until now.

I very specifically engaged the parishioners in reflection on the story of their church via homilies, meetings after our worship time, and prayers of intercession that named our dilemmas and asked for God's continued guidance. I noted in the gospel stories such things as opportunities, crises events, or people taking risks, and then invited the parishioners to name and describe an event in their parish life that had some of the same elements. I engaged them in these conversations because by now I was very conscious of the fact that they had great difficulty connecting their little church life to the larger church beyond themselves.[1]

In aligning the congregation's story with the practice of spiritual discernment, Ellen reflects on the particular movement of rooting with tradition:

> Rooting in tradition is meant to help the group form a "corporate memory" or get on the same page with their history. There seems to be a general myth in congregations that "everyone knows the story," which generally is not true. "Everyone has a piece of the story"—even if it is a story about what happened at church last Sunday.
>
> The rooting movement [in spiritual discernment] proved to be an eye-opening experience for the Montana congregation. They discovered how much hard work went into the founding of their church—not only the physical labor of constructing and maintaining the building and grounds, but the spiritual energy that went into securing missionaries for periodic liturgical services. Then, too, the early parishioners worked hard at sustaining their spiritual level by ministering to each other during times of great hardship.
>
> Storytelling in spiritual discernment calls for putting all the pieces of the story together, so that everyone knows the "thicker" story. It is then that biblical and theological reflection on the story can help the congregation understand itself—its priorities and values. When we wove the Montana congregation's story with the scripture stories of the lectionary, the parishioners began to see that they were not living out of their founding story. They had let go of some enthusiasm for a spiritual life together. Their values were focused on themselves. As we reflected on Luke 4:16–21, they saw that they were not open to concern for the poor, the stranger, the unwanted, and the marginalized of society as an integral part of living out the mission of Jesus.[2]

Returning to Ellen's story, we see how the Reed Point mission came to embrace its own history, myths and all.

Our conversations slowly began to surface some hopes the parishioners harbored about the church's viability, such as their expectation that they would always be taken care of regardless of their investment in the church. The conversations also uncovered some myths that had lingered on in their collective memory for years. If, in fact, some aspects of theses myths were true, whatever truth they had once contained was no longer visible.

During Advent we talked more in depth about the birth of this faith community. Then we moved on to tell about some Epiphany moments in its history (The eventual purchase of stained glass windows, for example). During Ordinary Time, we talked about the years of seeming stability, acknowledging how the church even contributed to the town's growth. During Lent we reflected seriously on the mystery of death, on what it means to personally die to our own desires for the sake of the common good. During Easter and Pentecost we spoke of rising to new life in Jesus Christ and our need to rely on God's spirit for sustenance and direction.

Gradually unspoken feelings of anger and betrayal (generally focused on the diocese, the bishop, and me for calling their parish life into question) began to surface. However, I still found the lectionary most helpful as a common focus, because we were using what was deeply intrinsic to our worship life—not a process that called for debate or invited hidden agendas—to construct our conversations and move us forward toward some decision about the church's future.

During the second Lenten season, the parishioners came to name and claim the decline of their church as their own responsibility. The oldest member even said publicly, "Sister, you're not to blame for this situation. We've known this was coming." That was a poignant moment. Her naming of the reality made it all okay—not pleasant, not welcome, but okay. Now this small group of parishioners could begin to let go of the past and take hold of their present situation.[3]

The process of patient, prayerful, spiritual discernment calls those who engage in the practice to shed attachments, let go of comforting securities, and relinquish what blocks God's gifts to them. This mission community gradually heard that call, as Sister Ellen describes.

> When challenged to let go of or release some of their own desires and fears, the congregation in Montana found it much more comfortable to be quietly introspective, or to retort by placing blame for the church's decline elsewhere. It is difficult to confront and name what needs to die in us so that we might allow God the room to do something new. Thus, it was important to me that I not rush the pace of their relinquishment. It was slow, like life naturally is in rural communities.
>
> For quite a long time, the parishioners avoided talking about the present and attempted to keep on living in the "glory days" of the past. But eventually time caught up. Maybe, as Bonhoeffer suggests, the community of Christ can only really be formed when some of its hopes and dreams have been shattered.[4]

Sister Ellen explains, "When the Montana congregation engaged in 'improving' the two options they were considering, they discovered a third option: close the church building and invite each parishioner to choose which one of the other two churches to join. (There were no local ecumenical options; their church was the only one in town.) . . . Once the parishioners talked and prayed more about those options, it was time to come to some closure."[5] They chose the third option. Sister Ellen commented, "Acting on this option would be difficult, but it also seemed to them to be the most spiritually life-giving."[6]

The church knew that sooner or later they would need to make a decision and move into a preferred future.

The decision that this mission church needed to close was made by the parishioners one Saturday evening, but the process of spiritual discernment was far from over. The few active parishioners who wanted to continue as members of a parish needed to be able to call some parish "home." So I initiated conversations with councils of both neighboring parishes—35 miles east and 35 miles west. (Meetings and bulletin inserts had already been used to keep their members informed of the evolving situation at the mission church.) The faith community at the mother church (where I ministered) was more understanding of the situation than the other community, which was less able to put itself in the other's shoes.[7]

The use of liturgies familiar to a faith community can be a real gift to them at a time when emotions rub raw and grief settles in. Reed Point mission claimed those. Ellen continues:

The last worship service at the mission church was held on Good Friday. Following the prescribed ritual and then a period of tearful silence, we removed the tabernacle, crucifix, lectern, altar, and then the cross that hung on the outside of the building. The altar stone was removed (as is customary; it is archived at the mother church), and the altar was dismantled, then buried. Then the doors of the church were closed and locked. As the ritual concluded, those present announced the name of the parish they would be joining on Easter Sunday.

On Easter Sunday, a few small sacred items from the former mission church were carried in procession into the two houses of worship, and following the liturgy, every new member was personally welcomed at receptions in the parish halls.[8]

As Sister Ellen later reflected on the closing, "The Montana congregation ritualized, in very significant ways during the seasons of

Lent and Easter, its own coming to rest on a very difficult decision. That decision still seems to have been God's yearning."[9]

This is indeed a sacred story—a story of life, decline, death, and new life. It is a story of denial, anger, great grief, closure, and eventual rebirth. The Word of God, opened and shared, helped reveal God's plan for this small congregation.

When faith communities in the twenty-first century actively grapple with what God's intentions might be for their future, the church's lectionary readings keyed to respective church seasons can provide an appropriate and challenging means—as well as spiritual energy—to help parishioners face their future together. While walking through the valleys of the shadow in Lent and bombarded with the craziness of human misbehavior in Holy Week, they can finally celebrate the grace and power of God in the new life of Easter faith.

ARE WE DEAD YET?
An Eastertide Story from
Trinity Lutheran Church, Omaha, Nebraska

The story of Trinity Lutheran Church can be placed squarely in Eastertide.[10] Their compelling communal question in 2000 centered on whether they had enough life in them to survive or would continue to decline and eventually die. The fear of possible death further paralyzed them and sapped their dwindling spirit. But a resurrection-like event infused them with new life, allowing them to look to the future with hope. Just as Christ had risen indeed, they were alive indeed! What happened? Hear their story.

In 1915 a group of Swedish immigrants who settled in Omaha gathered to form a new worshiping community. They initially assembled in homes, but within a few years grew in number and were able to construct a large church on Thirtieth Street in North Omaha. After worshiping for several years in their native Swedish tongue, they soon faced their first important decision—whether to worship in English. Now, nearly a century later, a Sudanese congregation that holds worship services in their building faces the same issue. Often the founding stories of a congregation repeat themselves.

The neighborhood surrounding the church certainly has changed because of racial, social, and economic transitions that have taken place over the years. The congregation was once the center of neighborhood activity, sponsoring significant social, youth, music, and athletic activities for its own members and the community at large. Some of the current members are fourth generation Trinity church folks and can tell stories about those good old days.

Eventually, those good old days ended. In the turbulent 1960s, the church lost its sense of unity that had been rooted in their ethnic identity as issues in society and the world at large affected the congregation. Members were leaving the neighborhood and moving further out into the suburbs of Omaha. Some members left the church over an internal rift. A long pastorate was accompanied by declining numbers and vitality. Around the turn of the century a new pastor, who was selected from the existing staff, was thrust into a difficult leadership role. Eventually he stumbled onto an evaluation tool and revitalization process that led to new life for the church. This congregation's story during a six-year period—from 2002 to 2007—can be placed squarely in the season of Eastertide.

When Pastor Mike Knudson was called to be the senior pastor of Trinity Lutheran Church, he felt ill-equipped to lead, given the congregation's slipping attendance. He began to panic and grasped at programmatic straws. Being a mainline Lutheran, he searched for resources within his own tradition and also explored outside resources and models for church growth and development. He tried various new initiatives, but they had minimal impact on the life and spirit of the congregation. He finally determined to use a sabbatical to search for potential help anywhere he could find it. On a personal level, he also sensed that he needed to become what he called a "radiating influence" as a pastor if he were to make a difference.

His search took him beyond the mainline church into areas he would normally have avoided. He held disdain for popular megachurch formulas, such as those of Willow Creek Community Church in the Chicago area. But eventually he found himself in one of their conferences with a chip on his shoulder, in effect announcing, "I dare you to influence me." In an informal time among conference participants at a hotel, he met and sat around a table with a group of Canadians to whom he told his story. They responded, "You are Lutheran. Natural Church Development is right up your alley." They explained why it could be right for him and his church. Natural Church Development (NCD) rose out of German religious culture, worked effectively with mainline churches, espoused trinitarian theology, and concentrated on building a healthy root system in the church rather than focusing on the fruits of growth—as did many church growth models. He began to investigate, for he was looking for a practical and effective tool that would enhance his own leadership and enable the church to look seriously at its decline and lack of vitality.

In investigating NCD, he learned that NCD is a set of growth principles and a process of self-evaluation developed by a German, Christian Schwarz, based on research with fifty thousand churches around the world and the United States.[11] Eight "quality characteristics" of healthy and productive churches have been isolated and included in a survey instrument that congregations can use to take their own spiritual and emotional temperature.

1. Empowering Leadership (Leadership is shared.)
2. Gift-oriented Ministry (Members serve based on their God-given strengths.)

3. Passionate Spirituality (Participation in church is based on love for God more than duty to God.)
4. Functional Structures (The organization is flexible enough to meet current needs, rather than being tradition bound.)
5. Inspiring Worship Services (Even when having fun, people can sense God's presence.)
6. Holistic Small Groups (People belong to a group where they can be the church for each other.)
7. Need-oriented Evangelism (The church knows the community and tailors its evangelism initiatives accordingly.)
8. Loving Relationships (New people are invited into relationship within an atmosphere of joy and trust.)

The program emphasizes the quality and health of the root system of the church rather than the fruit of numbers. Each church is urged to identify its unique individuality and embrace creativity, authenticity, and diversity, while remaining faithful to biblical concepts and a theological trinitarian compass.

After Pastor Mike shared his discovery with the Trinity church council, the council authorized initiating the NCD program, and a representative group of thirty knowledgeable members was chosen to respond to the NCD survey. The survey was scored by the NCD leadership, and the results were made available to the council and congregation. This survey would be repeated annually to provide a basis for new initiatives and a measuring stick for growth and transformation. Each one of the eight characteristics was scored on a numerical scale so that the leadership could see where they were strong and where they were weak. The scoring is not based on a percentile measured against some ideal standard but on an open-ended scale. A score of 50 is a median score, meaning that half of the churches in a given country scored lower and half scored higher on that characteristic. A score of 65 is considered a high score. Scoring in the low 30 range would indicate a path toward the valley of the shadow of death. Each characteristic might be pictured as a wooden stave forming a barrel. The barrel will only hold water to the height of the shortest stave. The survey at Trinity Lutheran Church revealed the following results, listed from highest to lowest score:

> Empowering Leadership: 48
> Loving Relationships: 43
> Gift-oriented Ministry: 42
> Functional Structures: 39
> Holistic Small Groups: 38
> Passionate Spirituality: 34
> Inspiring Worship: 32
> Need-oriented Evangelism: 31

The council and pastor heard alarm bells going off, since many of the scores were close to the death knell score of 30 points. They arranged for a series of cottage meetings for the congregation to discuss the findings. They also convened a gathering in which the people could form and review the corporate story of their congregation, using a timeline. Written on a long strip of paper mounted on the wall, the timeline was positioned where all could see it, add information to it, and reflect on it. Folks could see their ups and downs across the years and realized that they were on a track toward death.

The council determined that they needed a new group—what Pastor Mike referred to as a "proto-church renewal team"—to propose initiatives that would address the questions and needs the survey had exposed. At a general meeting with folks gathered around tables, members were asked to identify potential members for a new group. They were asked, "To whom would you entrust the future of this church, given the fact that the church may die?" Twelve names were suggested—and none of them were current members of the church council.

The first meeting of the renewal team produced a moment of awareness that indicated that God was active in this process. The members looked at each other and collectively seemed to say, "We are the ones whom God has chosen and to whom the congregation is looking to lead us out of this dire situation." Over several weeks of group formation, they met regularly to discuss a book on change that they were all reading. Every time they assembled, they asked one another, "What is really needed in this congregation at this time?"

They began to look at the scores on the survey and took their cue from those areas that needed to be immediately considered. Addressing the need for *inspiring worship* was an obvious choice, given how central that is to the life of a faith community. It became one of the first challenges for the new renewal team. They, along with the council and pastoral staff, were confronted with their own prejudice about how worship was to be designed and conducted. Each held a particular investment in their own familiar way of worship. They realized that they had to loosen a grip on personal preferences and grant permission to experiment with a much wider variety of worship styles if they were to hold onto their present members and attract new ones who may not be familiar with the Lutheran liturgies. They recognized that one size does not fit all and that they would need to offer more diverse opportunities for worship. This would be a new experience for them.

The renewal team explored a wide variety of worship styles, some that were foreign to the established members of the church. Then a new schedule of worship was introduced. A Thursday night service with contemporary music was designed to appeal particularly to people in their twenties and thirties. A family "new life" service with guitar accents was added to the Sunday morning schedule at 9:45, between an 8:30 traditional liturgy and an 11:00 blended service.

Realizing that some established members might be uncomfortable with unfamiliar worship patterns and schedules, the leaders followed the adage, "When the stress in the congregation increases, increase the pastoral care." They allayed many fears by offering opportunities for people to gather around dinners to tell their stories and discuss their new experiences of worship. In so doing, any negativity that might have built up was dissipated.

The renewal team visibly embraced diversity in worship by asking worship leaders to include in every worship service prayers of support for the other services. Representatives of the renewal team personally demonstrated their love for the people by being present in each worship service to lead the closing prayer. They blessed each service, asking for God's help in each particular one. They also held the prayer concerns and thanksgivings of the whole church before each worshiping community. These prayers came from the heart of trusted leaders and made a huge impact.

The congregation's investment and participation in worship—because of its centrality and visibility in the church's life—became the foremost subject for attention. The survey revealed that between 2002 and 2007, the *inspiring worship* score had jumped from 32 to 52. Several changes were welcomed, but presented another set of challenges. The Thursday evening service was successful for about five years. The younger people who had originally attended it moved further away from the church or began to have children, so a weekday evening service did not work for them. Attendance at the early morning liturgy declined due to an aging constituency and lessening interest. The timing of the family service presented challenges for the education and music programs. But it would have been difficult for the leaders in the congregation to envision going back to the way things were before. New life had been tasted and spirits had been refreshed.

The *passionate spirituality* score, although it increased from 31 in 2002 to 49 in 2007, still ranked lowest in both surveys. The issue had been addressed in worship and by introducing Bible study opportunities. A liturgical Lutheran tradition combined with a northern European Scandinavian reserve undoubtedly held that score down and remains a challenge.

The score for *need-oriented evangelism* actually doubled from 31 (the lowest score) in 2002 to 62 in 2007. Over that period the congregation made repeated attempts to connect with residents of a changing and decaying neighborhood of older homes that surrounded the church building. One sign of the outward focus occurred during the Christmas season when members of the renewal team assumed roles for an outdoor nativity scene. A passerby on foot stopped for conversation and asked if he could go inside the church to get warm. He became the first of many people struggling to meet basic survival needs to connect with the church in its new posture. That neighbors repeatedly sought out the congregation signaled the church was on a new track.

The pastoral staff began to make cold evangelism calls in the neighborhood and became known to a larger circle of people. A preschool began to operate in the church building and gathered children in the chapel for music daily. The building was offered to a not-for-profit group for a summer program that embraced about 150 African American girls in its activities. A Sudanese congregation worships in the church while maintaining its own customs and language. At Christmas, special ministries are focused on the surrounding increasingly Hispanic neighborhood.

Following Pastor Mike's departure for a call to another church, the parsonage was examined to determine whether it should be sold as it was or renovated. The council decided to spend twenty thousand dollars on the house as an investment in the neighborhood in order to attract a potential buyer who would maintain it with pride in the area. The house did sell, and the new buyer spent at least that much for additional improvements. He, along with the council, believed that every little bit of investment halts neighborhood decay and invites even more investment and improvements.

The score for *loving relationships* increased from 33 in 2002 to 66 in 2007, leading all categories in the survey. From its early days and continuing through its history, Trinity Lutheran Church had prided itself in being a close family church, especially when sports teams and music groups involving neighborhood residents crowded the calendar schedule. Scandinavian hospitality and food, part of its own community DNA, had been affirmed in the 2002 survey, but even that improved.

Holistic small groups also showed an increase from 38 to 58. A number of small support or study groups had been spawned but had a limited life span. The church leaders learned something about the life cycle of small groups but discovered something more—that ongoing groups in every facet of church life were important organs in the body of the church. Examination of the church's website reveals the existence of a dozen life situation groups; service, mission, youth, music, and Bible study groups; and more. The fact that they are described on the website indicates how prominent they are in the social conscience of the church.[12]

When Trinity Lutheran Church was formed and named nearly a century ago, few would have been able to forecast how they were to live out their religious practice as Trinity church. They do have a large stained glass window depicting the Trinity. They could have foreseen the bright lights of Advent growth and the Christmas celebration of God's love. But few would have foreseen their walk through the valley of the shadow of death on Good Friday and the wake-up call on resurrection morn to be really alive. Their experience made Trinity come alive for them.

The Natural Church Development program in which they have been engaged affirms the theological and strategic centrality of the Trinity. They orient themselves using a trinitarian compass in order to grow the church deep into its roots. Various congregations that utilize the NCD program describe their journey along different paths, but each finds that if they live out of deep, nourishing roots, they will produce fruit in a natural and healthy way. NCD's promotional and interpretive material states, "Applying the Trinitarian compass brings balance—to the life of individual believers and whole churches. . . . It releases an almost magnetic attraction that is far more powerful than all of the marketing techniques. . . . People notice that they are drawn closer and closer to the living God."[13]

The story of Trinity Lutheran Church cannot be told apart from the spiritual journeys of the leadership core of the congregation. The role of the senior pastor was critical to moving the congregation into a renewal mode. He threw a pebble into the pond, sending ripples that reached the shoreline of the neighborhood. Pastor Mike had served Trinity as an associate pastor until he was called to the senior pastor role upon a long-tenured pastor's retirement. His selection set up a crisis in leadership—both for him personally and for the congregation. He was tentative and uncertain. They had grown accustomed to a familiar leadership style. Both knew the congregation was in decline and hurting, and its future was uncertain. But could the youthful abilities and ambitions of a new leader be enough to pull them out of it?

The move into a new leadership role set up a crisis in faith for Pastor Mike. He was unsettled and uncertain about his own leadership abilities. His discomfort intensified with a diagnosis of lung cancer in December 2000. These two factors conspired to produce the faith crisis. He sensed that he was drifting from God's presence and was in no position to lead from a deep spiritual well.

When Pastor Mike introduced the NCD program to the church he knew that it carried additional risks for him personally. The program might bomb. He would be out front as a leader with even more at stake spiritually and emotionally than if he had tried to prop up a declining congregation out of his own limited resources. The survey had produced a wake-up call for the church and that added to the pressure he felt to produce and lead. What if they would not respond?

The survey instrument's results and follow-up process made a world of difference in his self-awareness as a leader. Before the process, if anyone had asked him if he was a leader, he would have hemmed and hawed. He had been more comfortable in an associate role. Now through the support of a tried and true program, he could take risks and lead by example—even when the result might be uncertain. And he could lead by proposing responses that could help the congregation face hard questions and tackle big challenges. The opportunity to fly with new wings energized him. Training in a specific program provided the support and energy he needed for setting up the NCD program and working with folks, eventually creating proposals for revitalization that could lead them beyond the question, "Are we dead yet?"

After the survey of the congregation and the first round of discussion sessions with the congregation, he found that his leadership role energized his faith. This self-realization became a real epiphany for him. While working with the renewal team in the midst of the congregation's progress in the eight critical areas of its corporate life, he saw more clearly that he was to play a vital role to keep the congregation alive and inspired. He did indeed see his pastoral role as a radiating influence. Early in this process he became aware that they all were moving together out of fear and into faith. It happened in a "millisecond," he said, calling it "realized eschatology." Even though the congregation still had a lot to work through, something substantive had changed. Victory had come to them in the moment, and they would not have to wait until a future budget would be pledged or the church would grow. They could proclaim, "Christ is risen and we are alive indeed!"

One sign that Pastor Mike was experiencing a personal transformation arose from his increasing comfort level with the term *Lord*. Prior to the church initiative, the term made him uncomfortable. But through the varied worship experiences, he came to embrace an affectionate and intimate God as "Lord" rather than a hierarchical and distant God.

The staff, which consisted of pastors, musicians, educators, and support personnel and who had to work together to respond to the many new challenges with new skills, discovered that the eight qualities identified by NCD also applied to their common life. When they met regularly in a room together they found a deepening appreciation for and trust in one another, cherishing rather than judging. Communal prayer became an integral part of their ongoing life.

Through all the initiatives and transitions, tension between the council and renewal team was minimal. They functioned together in faith, hope, and love. The challenges before both groups were to focus on "what needs help now" as they worked together to address the very specific needs that each year's survey surfaced. They worked in an integrated fashion in what could have been an endless competitive tug-of-war. The 2007 survey revealed a score increase from 48 in 2002 to 61 for *empowering leadership.*

Tangible evidence that the spirit of God was at work in the congregation's call to self-assessment and renewal came in the form of an unexpected gift—a miracle of life. An angel from afar, who was not a member of the church, became aware of the path the church was taking. She had grown up in a nearby Omaha neighborhood, and decided that she wanted to support the effort. She contributed a one-time gift of twenty-five thousand dollars. The council wisely responded by creating a renewal fund for the renewal team's use, rather than depending on a budget line that might get lost within a general budget. That fund encouraged and empowered the team to plan creatively. It proved to be a God-sent resource that was used for specific initiatives over the first several years of the NCD program.

The seasonal connection with Eastertide in Trinity Lutheran Church's story leads us to consider the postresurrection ministry of Jesus as a leader with radiating influence. In his postresurrection appearances, Jesus tended to his followers' deep feelings of fear and doubt. He reassured them with repeated "Don't be afraid" counsel and visited them at opportune moments. On a road to Emmaus, he talked with two disciples about their experiences and concerns. Later that day he revealed himself to them in the breaking of bread.

In a closed room, he invited Thomas to touch his wounds. In Galilee he helped frustrated fisherman find a school of fish. Around a charcoal fire and fish breakfast, he restored Peter and all of the disciples into a loving relationship with himself and with one another. His Great Commission pointed them to a future.

Jesus built and tended a healthy body life among his followers. His ministry pattern in postresurrection appearances becomes a good model for leaders of congregations in the midst of their own Eastertide story, while proclaiming, "We are not dead yet. We are risen, indeed!"

CHAPTER 6

The Pentecost Triad
in Churches Named Trinity

Sometimes called the "lost season," the ten-day period that precedes the festival of Pentecost is frequently overlooked because of a hangover from Easter or the hustle and bustle of the early summer season. Yet the days are distinct and important in the stories of congregations. Jesus instructed his disciples to wait and pray during the time following his ascension. We would rather get on with the program. But sometimes we may need to choose to call time-out on our own and go on an intentional retreat into silent waiting. At other times the circumstances of our story force us to our knees to wait in prayerful anticipation.

While the ten-day period of waiting is the shortest season of the church year, the post-Pentecost season is the longest—beginning in June and closing with the celebration of Christ the King Sunday in late November. That is the season for the growing and greening of the church and for its mission for justice, peace, and witness in the world, culminating with the affirmation that Jesus is Lord of all. The next two congregational stories are associated with the triad of the pre- and post-Pentecost festival.

A SEASON OF PURPOSEFUL STILLNESS
A Pre-Pentecost Story from
Trinity Church, Omaha, Nebraska

Trinity Church is a large, independent, evangelical church located along a busy thoroughfare in the growing western section of Omaha, Nebraska.[1] Historically, they have attempted to live out their name by embracing both the lordship of Jesus and the power of the Holy Spirit. They invite their members to come to Jesus as Savior and Lord, counting the cost and relying on the comforting and powerful presence of the Holy Spirit. They believe that life in Christ is to be facilitated by the power of the Holy Spirit and the two need to be experienced together, lest separating the two would produce fanaticism or even spiritual death.

Historically, the congregation was connected to the Christian Missionary Alliance tradition and came into existence through several church splits from the Gospel Tabernacle mother church in downtown Omaha, where gifts of the Spirit were fostered and celebrated. They were solidly trinitarian in their beliefs, but over the years this orthodoxy became rigid and unloving.

When the founding pastor retired in 1996, he handpicked the new pastor from the existing staff. Under the leadership of the new pastor, worship services took on an appealing evangelical character, and church attendance soared to 2,800 while financial contributions followed suit. Twenty percent of the contributions were budgeted for outreach beyond the church. The church's story at this point could be likened to the early ministry of Jesus in Galilee—growth and popularity. Trinity became known as a flagship church in the evangelical community of Omaha.

A recent season of Trinity Church, however, can be compared to the post-Ascension days leading up to Pentecost. Just as Jesus's disciples followed his instruction to wait and pray for the gift of the Spirit, the members of Trinity entered a season of intentional stillness. They had endured a difficult time around leadership issues and variant visions, which resulted in a number of staff members leaving the church. Church attendance dropped from 2,800 to 1,500 worshipers. While working through some incredibly challenging circumstances and facing significant spiritual battles that could be compared to Lenten and Holy Week struggles, the remaining church leadership fastened onto two biblical images that nurtured them through the crisis and positioned their unfolding story in the pre-Pentecost season.

They drew the first biblical image from Isaiah's message to King Hezekiah regarding Assyria's threats against the kingdom of Judah: "And this shall be the sign for you: This year you shall eat what grows of itself, and in the second year what springs from that; then in the third year sow, reap, plant vineyards, and eat their fruit. The surviving remnant of the house of Judah shall again take root downward, and bear fruit upward; for from Jerusalem a remnant shall go out, and from Mount Zion a band of survivors. The zeal of the LORD of hosts will do this" (2 Kings 19:29–31). This story became important to Trinity Church. It gave them permission to slow down and relinquish their impulse to frantically generate outreach programs to make up for their losses. And it invited them to put down deep roots that would eventually produce good fruit.

The second image came from the Song of Solomon: "Arise, my love, . . . and come away; for now the winter is past, the rain is over and gone. The flowers appear on the earth; the time of singing has come" (Song of Sol. 2:10–12). The text named the time they were in. It was winter and an opportunity for a rainy season. They looked forward to the days of spring and the blooming of new initiatives. But those blessings would have to wait. They needed to remain idle and allow the rain to soak in.

During a two-year season of "taking root downward," the church chose not to focus its energies on evangelism and outreach but rather to build relationships within its own community. In this time of intentional stillness, church members chose to embrace their own suffering and to acknowledge that, in some ways, they had grieved the Holy Spirit. They connected their experience to the sufferings of Christ. They allowed for tears and openly encouraged the practice of lamenting in their common life, admitting that crying can be life giving. They stood by the senior pastor, who had become a focal point in their church conflict. They walked alongside both him and his wife in their journey through cancer treatment. They affirmed that authentic living embraces suffering. Yes, they prayed for the gift of healing for the pastor, the staff, and themselves, even while living with the knowledge that healing may not come. A recent series of worship themes and study opportunities focused on what it means to be emotionally healthy and spiritually mature, not only as individuals but also as a congregation.

People are invited to come to the church and be honest about their feelings and life experiences. Through Trinity's LIFEcare ministry of pastoral care and biblical counseling, staff members help people recognize the seasons of their own lives. As the church attempts to rebuild the house, they ask God to make them capable of caring for others—especially those who hurt.

The website for Trinity Church presents this caring posture to the inquiring community: "Trinity is an interdenominational church with twelve pastors from various Evangelical backgrounds and as a church we represent a wide spectrum of Evangelical theology. Sit in a really safe place to hear a really dangerous message." As a result of the congregation's embrace of their own wounding, tears, and suffering, visitors pick up the difference between honest admission and cool denial. One sensitive and discerning woman, who had encountered an unusual amount of ugliness in her past church experience and who had vowed never to come close to situations like that again, attested to actually feeling the lack of tension at Trinity. This was a significant observation, given the amount of tension the congregation had experienced in recent years.

Within the staff, a deep sense of love, trust, and humility emerged. They realized they needed each other's gifts in ministry as well as emotional and spiritual support in order to lead the congregation and help it heal and grow. As leaders they strove to honor those who were in authority and even have their own pet projects laid aside if need be so that the congregation could put its resources into more appropriate initiatives. They acknowledged spiritual warfare in their midst and attempted to defy the enemy by overcoming it with the integrity that love brings. As one staff member said, "It was more important to be loving than to be right." Through the struggle and grieving, they realized that the path of love is life giving. While on this learning path, they intentionally practiced not being controlled by what others—especially outsiders—may think. Nourishing relationships were also claimed in the wider religious community. Trinity's difficulties were well known in Omaha's church circles and beyond. Pastors in other congregations of the city, realizing that Trinity had taken a hit, came to pray with and support the staff.

While the attendance now numbers about fifteen hundred worshipers, not counting children, the leaders have embraced a new common vision to train and equip five hundred of their worshiping members to be committed disciples within 2009. Deepening their roots to become effective disciples has trumped the attendance-numbers game.

Of all the emerging dynamics in this season of intentional stillness, the practices of worship have returned the congregation to its ecclesiastical rooting in the presence of the Holy Spirit. Like many megachurches, Trinity has a long-standing practice of planning every detail of its worship services and using various media to communicate its message. Trinity's leaders continue to design and plan worship well. They think and plan strategically, but now do so with a new twist. They do "creative worship service planning in an uncertain atmosphere." In other words, they are willing to allow the Lord to mess with their plans. They are willing to stop the flow of the service to allow the Holy Spirit to work through their plans or even to subvert them. This openness to the winds of the Spirit allows them to assume a posture somewhat like the disciples' ten days of pre-Pentecost waiting and yearning in the upper room that Luke describes in Acts 1. Services have been stopped, for instance, to focus on single moms, inviting them to come forward and be surrounded by the prayers of the people, or to focus on unemployed people, linking them with people who had job contacts or gifts related to job hunting. If they had not paused in their pre-Pentecost journey to determine that they would intentionally respond to interruptions like these, they would not have been able to enter into the ministry of the full season of Pentecost.

Trinity's worship leaders are open to the gift of prophecy in which a person may speak under the influence of the Spirit. They do not open the microphone to anyone who wants to speak but only to those whom they have discerned to have the gifts of wisdom and sensitivity. Prophecy and freedom to speak are both subject to the spirit of wise discernment. The church website proclaims:

> We believe we offer a safe, secure environment to hear a potentially dangerous message; one that invites the Holy Spirit to "show up" whenever, wherever and however He chooses, but with confident, healthy leadership that doesn't allow things to get out of control. . . .
>
> When you come to Trinity, you can expect a LIFE-giving experience marked by:
>
> • Creativity without anxiety or stress, for the team or the congregation
> • Hearing about, seeing and experiencing the love, presence, and power of the Holy Spirit

- Leaders with courage and humility, willing to step out in faith while always grounding themselves in God's Word and with a heart for people
- Messages that connect with you, but don't let you stay comfortable with the "status quo" in your own life or in the life of your community
- Prayers for healing that release faith in everyone who hears or receives them
- Worship about Him and for Him, but that also ministers to people[2]

As we look into the narrative of Trinity Church, we see a church on a pilgrimage. They have walked through the seasons of waiting and yearning that called for letting go. Their Advent season can be seen through the founding stories of planning, while celebrating the love of God in the gift of Jesus. Their Lenten season can be seen through disruptive stories of uncertainty, division, and struggle that drew them to God's presence as Suffering Servant. But they survived and claimed the Easter good news. "We are risen indeed."

And now they are called again into relinquishment and letting go in this current season of pre-Pentecost waiting and yearning. They are deepening their roots into serious and costly discipleship, all the while anticipating the presence of the Spirit, who will help them plant and grow the kingdom. They wait in purposeful stillness—together in an upper room on the eve of Pentecost—where they have returned to their founding charism. That charism ties their identity to the presence and work of the Holy Spirit. It allows them to "sit in a really safe place to hear a really dangerous message." They are shedding some of their unhealthy spiritual DNA, holding on to all that is—and was—good, always seeking to be "built together spiritually into a dwelling place for God" (Eph. 2:22).

LET THE SILENCE DO THE HEAVY LIFTING
A Pentecost Story from Trinity
Episcopal Church, Independence, Missouri

Selecting Trinity Episcopal Church in Independence, Missouri, to depict the long season of Pentecost may seem odd, for by many measurements the church should be dead.[3] Founded in 1844 as the first Episcopal Church in the Kansas City area, it got off to a rocky start, managing to survive the turmoil of the Civil War. When Confederate troops invaded the city, their priest was jailed, while two people removed and hid important documents and furnishings from the church and most members fled.

It ministered out of a small but very beautiful building in the village of Independence until it was overwhelmed by the notoriety of being "the Truman church." Harry S. Truman and Bess Wallace were married in the church on June 18, 1919. Their daughter, Margaret, was also married there in 1956. The south wall of the sanctuary bears a plaque marking the pew where Harry and Bess regularly sat for worship. President Truman delivered a short address at the church in 1959 when a new wing was dedicated. Following his presidency, his legendary morning walks in Independence took him to familiar sites around town, including Trinity Church. The Trumans' fame brought four U.S. presidents into the sanctuary for special events. Bess Truman's funeral was held in that sacred space in 1982. The church library on the second floor of the new wing houses a large section of green bound folders that contain Bess's letters from Washington, D.C., and news clippings, photos, and programs of church events in which the Trumans were involved.

Trinity's legacy as the Truman church became the primary topic of conversation for visitors who attended. The sanctuary was redecorated to restore the simple beauty of this small church befitting its historic importance. But as the members aged, died, or moved away, it became a small, struggling church served only by short-term or temporary priests.

During the Truman years Trinity had the reputation of being a country club church; but in recent years Trinity found itself in a transitioning neighborhood at the edge of downtown, in a largely blue-collar, working-poor town. Furthermore, Independence is the national center for the Reformed Church of the Latter Day Saints, whose buildings dominate the community's skyline and culture. It did not appear to be a promising setting for an Episcopal church's redevelopment and expansion.

The church prospered during the Truman years and even survived the notoriety of being the Truman church, only to get caught up in national church politics when a gay clergyman, Eugene Robinson, was elected Episcopal bishop of New Hampshire. Many members left Trinity in protest. Its membership fell to forty-five, and their bishop doubted whether the church had a future. Temporary and interim leadership during this difficult time failed to help people process the changes they were facing, and the future of the church was precarious.

Trinity church's transformation into a lively, spiritually focused trinitarian community of faith began with the appointment of Mary Glover as priest. She was also an attorney. As priest, she ministered and taught out of a servant role. To quiet the controversy over Robinson's appointment, she said, "We will have three weeks of voicing opinions in an open forum. Then we will move on."

Some members also had qualms about women serving as clergy, which led to additional members leaving, but her self-perception as a servant made a big impact. She said, "If we trust God to do God's work, our own needs will be met." The parishioners fondly referred to her as "Mother Mary," and she seemed comfortable with their designation. She turned the church's attention to the surrounding community and recommended letting go of the four hundred dollars per month income generated by renting an adjacent building the church owned, and instead turning the building into a hospitality center for the poor and homeless. The vestry, in a genuine act of faith, approved the recommendation.

After several years, the Reverend Glover returned to Texas to tend her ailing mother, and a new rector, Father Sam Mason, was appointed. Whereas Trinity's few remaining members had once been more inclined to talk about the past rather than a potential future, which tended to imprison the church, these two rectors had begun to slowly change the way people talked about the church. They began to talk about its future life and mission. In two years the church grew from 45 to 140 members. Its ministries extended into the neighboring community. Its story connects with the season of Pentecost because of the outbreak of new ministries. The church bubbled with Pentecost energy. What made the difference?

Father Mason had been a rough and tough young man, having been a rodeo clown, football player, and military gunner. He had also been raised Anglican and was familiar with the prayer book and other resources for faith development. His mother taught him to never run from difficulties in the church. "No matter what happens, remember this is your church," she insisted. Those seeds were used by the Spirit to prompt his call to ministry. While serving in Operation Desert Storm, the first Gulf War, he and a Lutheran friend vowed to God and to one another that if they did not have to kill anyone, they would become clergymen. They did not have to kill, and after the war, they presented themselves to their respective surprised bishops as candidates for ordained ministry. Sam's awareness that the Holy Spirit worked beyond normal expectations, along with his own natural abilities and assertiveness served him well in his new assignment to Trinity church.

He soon learned the importance of the name Trinity. Instead of dismissing the reference as ordinary or mundane, he chose to embrace the name. He had come from a tradition that emphasized the importance of being "in Christ." Now he was forced to consider the whole Trinity as a way of living out the gospel. He took a new look at the Jewish tradition and boned up on the witness of the Old Testament scriptures. He realized that the psalms laid a foundation for the New Testament. He revisited the dynamic work of the Holy Spirit in the life of the early Christian church. As the spiritual leader of this church, he would attempt to bring a trinitarian awareness to match its name and heritage. The mission of the church would be to help people find God in the presence of Christ while being empowered by the Holy Spirit. The renewed trinitarian orientation would be expressed not only in words but also in works.

When church members began to catch hold of the freshness and power of embracing the name Trinity, some said, "We wish we had been named after a saint. It would have been easier!" They could have more easily grasped the presence of God represented by a mere human. But the name Trinity invited them into the very nature of the love, grace, and power of God. Who could comprehend that? Who could live into that relationship?

How did they begin embracing their name Trinity? Father Sam said, "We did it in the 'snooty' old Episcopal way. We did it with traditional liturgy and community life!" They rebuilt their life by inviting people to know Christ through the witness of the Holy Spirit. In liturgy they offer the traditional Holy Eucharist Rite One at 8:00 and a family Eucharist using contemporary Rite Two at 10:30 on Sunday mornings. Within the liturgy, people are given the opportunity to express how "God is with me." These testimonies led some to consider putting together a diary of these accounts to capture the witnesses' excitement.

The passing of the peace—which had been difficult for these Episcopalians—is now one of the most significant parts of the liturgy. Greetings and embraces are exchanged. Birthdays and anniversaries are celebrated. Whereas worshipers at one time were more concerned to get out of church on time in order to make an athletic event, they now are willing to extend the service for this vital interaction, calling it one of the best times in the service.

An adult forum was inserted between services to consider spiritual, missional, or social issues that confront the larger denominational or ecumenical church. Folks who used to worship and then go out to breakfast now have opportunity over coffee to join others for a brief growth and fellowship experience. In addition, a potluck dinner followed by a service of evening prayer and healing at 6:00 p.m. on Wednesdays has been added. It provides a meaningful way for people in the community who have particular needs to stop by for a welcoming meal and prayer. Its regularity provides a right time for sudden needs and ongoing prayer to coincide.

Trinity Sunday, the first Sunday after Pentecost, has become one of the most significant feast days for the church—like a birthday or a naming party. One year several families who had been embroiled in a family feud and who had become inactive decided to get together, bury the hatchet, and become reconciled. They used the Trinity Sunday family potluck picnic as an occasion to demonstrate forgiveness, redemption, and healing. Their reconciliation became symbolic for the whole church.

But what is different about the liturgy? For the first time in ten years, they now have a choir for the family service. Those who attend worship notice the difference in the level of energy from the choir, from new younger members, from the celebrations and prayers, and from the leadership of the priest. Father Mason insists that the new energy is not tied to his persona. He says he is easy going, so the intensity does not come from him. He only lifts up God's presence by focusing on all three members of the Trinity. Living out the trinitarian life brings people into mystery and the awareness of the Holy Spirit's working. They see miracles that cannot be explained apart from God's activity in their midst. Father Sam likes to say that "the silence does the heavy lifting," that the Spirit works beyond their own efforts to accomplish what matters most in people's lives. The concept of the Trinity is now seen as an evangelical tool to be embraced and used.

Some members observed that what drew them to Trinity and held them together as a congregation in the past was a sense of guilt for their sins, followed by Jesus's forgiveness and release.

Now they are spiritually rooted in a relationship with the love of God, the grace of Jesus, and the power of the Holy Spirit. All their potential spiritual muscles had not been used because they were locked into only one person of the Trinity—Jesus Christ.

But what signs of the Trinity can be seen in the congregation's outward life and mission? If the Trinity were to be fully embraced, it would be evidenced in daily life. God's full presence would touch the world where people live and work. Besides significant growth in numbers and vitality for the congregation, several others signs can be noted:

- The budget was met last year—the first time in several years.
- Second floor rooms, which over the years gathered clutter and stuff, are being cleaned out and reclaimed as attractive space for a nursery and children's classrooms. Even though the numbers may be small, volunteers believe, like the character in *Field of Dreams,* "If we build it, they will come." One volunteer couple said, "We need kids!" They believed in a future and did something about it. The restoration and decorating work is being done by cancer survivors and those with arthritic hands.
- The Mustard Seed hospitality center next door to the church expanded and has become an attractive thrift shop. Staffed by volunteers, the shop raised over twenty thousand dollars last year to support mission efforts, in addition to offering low-priced goods to the poor of the town. People are able to obtain clothing and goods with dignity, even when items are given to them. Every morning the staff starts their day with prayers using the three names of the Trinity.
- The center director, Joan Spease, came to her role out of a significant faith journey. She had been an inactive member of Trinity until women of the church invited her to a welcoming brunch. The women introduced and invited her

into a "Spiritual Awakening Book Club." She accepted their invitation and began to participate. While there she began to experience the warmth of a faith family. That gift of grace was timely, for over the next several years she lost a daughter to cancer, a grandson to suicide, and a family home to fire. "I was numb," she said. "I could never have made it without the help of Trinity." Now she gives back through the ministry of the Mustard Seed. For instance, she welcomes and has established a relationship with a regular visitor to the thrift shop—a woman who brings her Alzheimer's-impaired mother into the shop, where she is given a doll. She welcomes a homeless and learning-challenged young man who has been rejected by his family because he is gay, but who now volunteers at the shop and sings in the choir. She personifies the hospitality of Christ to others who come into the Mustard Seed with special needs.

• For more than sixty years the church hosted and has led a Boy Scout program, even though the scouts are not associated with the church. In addition to conducting a Shrove Tuesday pancake feed for fifteen to eighteen hundred people, the Boy Scouts take on various service projects in the community on behalf of the church. The church has had plenty of excuses to discontinue its relationship, but the scouts' ongoing dedication makes each year seem like a new ministry.

• Eagle Scouts in the troop constructed a labyrinth in a large open area next to the parking lot behind the church. Its purpose was to provide a setting to teach the trinitarian presence of God to those who walked it. Young people regularly bring favorite rocks and stones to help line the border of the circling path. Two large trees offer shade to walkers who sit to rest and meditate on a bench at the labyrinth's center. The labyrinth is visible to people who go for walks in the neighborhood, and the public also uses it frequently.

In addition, walkers have a panoramic view of the historic courthouse, Truman landmarks, and the spires of the many churches of the city. In coming back out from the center of the labyrinth, those who walk are reminded of the larger world in which they are to witness and serve.

- One man who did not attend church detested the labyrinth and communicated his dismay to any who would listen— yet he could be seen walking it regularly. After some time he began to attend Alcoholics Anonymous meetings, then went into therapy, and is now recovering from his addiction. Something about walking the labyrinth draws people into the mystery of spiritual formation. They begin to release their addictions and whatever blocks God's grace, then rest in God's attentive love and grace. Eventually, they take hold of aspects of their life that they had formerly ignored or dismissed and live as responsible stewards in the world. Walkers do indeed meet the Trinity as they stand in awe and wonder of God's creation, Christ's forgiveness and call to follow him, and the Spirit's life-giving and healing powers. Trinity church is aware of the importance of the ways that God enters people's lives through sensory accents that touch the heart and soul. They want folks to be able to touch, smell, and feel God's presence. The labyrinth offers one sensory accent.

- With an aim to join the Trinity in ministry to the working poor of the city, Trinity Episcopal Church, in partnership with St. Mary's Roman Catholic Church, has helped eighty-five families from outside the church find housing and jobs. The church has assumed responsibility for providing an apartment at a cost of five thousand dollars per year for Hillcrest Ministries, a ministry to homeless and unemployed families. This ecumenically sponsored project offers a welcome, ninety days of lodging, and support for people who are making a transition from their broken lives.

- Outdoor worship and gatherings in the vicinity of the Mustard Seed thrift shop, the church parking lot, and the labyrinth offer an easy way for the community to discover the opportunities for worship and ministry that the church offers. When Gary Leado, a graduate of the diocese's lay academy, wanted to connect with the community, he gathered folks on Wednesday evenings for prayers of healing. When Father Sam came to Trinity, he added a potluck dinner. Laypeople lead the prayers, or if Eucharist is offered, the priest leads them. Gary and Sam have both realized that a surprising number of community people "just drop in."
- During an interview with Father Mason, I commented that after hearing the information about the supper and service on the church's answering phone, I really wanted to attend. It sounded so inviting! He responded, "I did not want the phone message to seem like many church announcements, so I redid it nine times before I was satisfied. I wanted it to really be an appealing invitation." My response and affirmation was taken as a blessing of the effort. It worked!

These are all outward signs of a church that is living out its name, Trinity. The season of Trinity Episcopal's current story is Pentecost—looking to a future instead of the past, becoming bold in witness, connecting to the hungry and poor, claiming the Spirit's presence, and allowing the Silence to do the lifting. Trinity's website offers a welcome to all who come through its doors:

If you are curious, look for answers here.
If you have been hurt, look for comfort here.
If you are joyous, look for us to join you in song.
If you are overwhelmed, look for peace.
If you are enthusiastic, come praise with us.
If you are energetic, join us in service to God's work.
If you don't fit in, see if there's a place for you here.

If you are lonely, look for companionship.

If you seek quiet, you can still be among us.

If you love God, find others who want to share that love with you.

If you don't much like God, take a look from a different point of view.[4]

As the church prepares to celebrate its 165th anniversary in 2009, its members will look back at their history and see three ways to name God's presence. They will reaffirm their identity as Trinity. They will look to a future investment in ministry within the congregation and in the community.

When Father Sam looked back at the history of the church and looked around to what is happening in this season of Pentecost, he summarized his observations to me in a personal conversation. "I like to call this embrace of Trinity 'mystical magic alive' or 'divine happenstance.' We are not doing it. God is."

The season of Pentecost is the longest in the church year. It invites the Christian community to be about the work of Jesus in the world from day to day and week to week. The time may seem ordinary, but it is filled with extraordinary evidences of God's presence. For Trinity church, preaching, teaching, healing, feeding, clothing, housing, and welcoming are all ongoing expressions of the love of God, the grace of Christ, and the power of the Spirit. The Trinity is the "silence that does the heavy lifting."

CHAPTER 7

Toward a New Story

In the previous three chapters we have seen congregational stories for each season that precedes and flows from the three major festivals of the church year—Christmas, Easter, and Pentecost. Each one of these churches is solidly connected with a specific church season and the wisdom inherent within it. While having introduced what I call the waltz of the gospel as a structure for understanding our own local stories, we recognize that congregational stories do not necessarily move through that waltz in a sequential order.

REFRAMING OLD STORIES

We may place our stories in a particular season, but as those stories unfold and develop, we may discern the need to move them to another season. Unexpected circumstances and interruptions in a smooth story line may lead us to jump from one to another. The very nature of the journey of faith presupposes an untidy sequence. Trinity Church, Omaha, moved from Lenten conflict to pre-Pentecost stillness. Holy Trinity Orthodox moved from Lenten death gasps to Advent waiting and finally into Pentecost. Trinity Episcopal of Independence moved from Eastertide life to Lenten distress to Pentecost fulfillment. Trinity Lutheran of Mission, Kansas, was well established in Epiphany and is being drawn into pre-Pentecost waiting to discern the shape of servanthood in Eastertide.

In the milieu of taking hold, Epiphany calls for boundary crossing, Eastertide calls for body building, and Pentecost calls for kingdom realization. Church stories will move back and forth between them. In the milieu of letting go, Advent calls for planning, Lent calls for resolving conflict and difficulties, and pre-Pentecost calls for concentrated readiness. Likewise, churches will adjust their attention accordingly.

The structure of the church year invites us to reframe our stories. Often churches get stuck in the story of one particular season and do not see the necessity of reframing their story for another season. So in looking at church stories in your setting, you will want to know with what seasons the church's story has connected in the past, in what season the church's story currently resides, and to what season the church's story is being drawn. Sudden conflict, for instance, will force a church into the Lenten season for clarification and resolution. Fragmentation or stagnation of the body will invite a visit to Eastertide for life, health, and energy. Hurdles and roadblocks may move the story across boundaries into Epiphany.

One purpose in laying out the church's seasons has been to aid you in entering into the tradition of Scripture—the story of God's creating, redemptive, and sanctifying initiatives in the world. In so doing, I have separated out strands of meaning that appear in the eternal rhythms of spiritual formation, letting go, naming God's presence, and taking hold. This triad can be found in each of the three major cycles of the church year. Each festival that marks God's presence is preceded by a waiting and yearning season and is followed by a proclaiming and sending season. When combined, they become the waltz of the gospel. Advent stories affected by the good news of God's love in Christmas may be reframed into Epiphany stories. Lenten stories into which new life of Easter resurrection has been breathed may be reframed into lively Eastertide stories. And pre-Pentecost stories infused by the Spirit may be reframed into powerful Pentecost stories.

Engaging in this dance through our stories and the seasons of the church year will form a trinitarian spirituality within us. Trinitarian spirituality is unique in that it associates the real experiences of our life with the workings of a trinitarian deity. The Trinity always functions in loving and harmonious relationships. Likewise, we will see that a story identified with a single season will have deeper meaning when it is seen in relationship to stories in other seasons that mark God's trinitarian presence along the spiritual journey. One step in the waltz is enriched by association with the other two steps. Dances consist of several interrelated steps. The expert dancer always adjusts to an unexpected step of the dance partner.

Although separating out the steps of a waltz of the gospel and associating them with particular seasons of the church year may help us understand and reflect theologically on our own stories, we may become confused as well. Steps of a waltz are well ordered, but each dancer brings a unique style and movement that may defy neat categories and definitions. Likewise, the Trinity defies neat formulas and frequently draws us into mystery. Just as the Trinity draws us into the mystery of interdependent relationships, so too our inability to fully grasp the Trinity may lead some to feel confused as they attempt to work with their own stories in a trinitarian context.

THE MYSTERY OF STORY IN TRINITY

Several years ago a presbytery invited me to spend the last half of a leadership training day to introduce a leadership development process that I was thinking about but had not used. The invitation was open ended. I had been thinking about the subject of this book—connecting church stories to the seasons of the church year—but had not written about the idea nor presented it to any groups. Now I had an invitation to experiment and to see how a group might respond. The environment would be safe and the participants willing. The presbytery leaders who had invited me supported my proposal.

I divided the fifty participants into groups of four people and gave each group an assignment. They were to number off one through four based on the order of their birthdates. Then I gave the groups their assignment along these lines:

> Number four, you are to tell the story of a significant event in your congregation, preferably within the past year. The rest of you are to listen but with ears tuned to particular messages. Number one, you are to put on the ears of the Christmas triad. Listen closely to the letting go of Advent, for signs of the presence of a loving and giving God in Christmas, and look for the light of boundary crossing in Epiphany. Number two, you are to put on the ears of the Easter triad. Listen for letting go in the tensions and difficulties of Lent, the grace and living presence of Jesus, and signs of taking hold to proclaim life-giving news in Eastertide. Number three, you are to put on the ears of the Pentecost triad. Listen for practices of centered prayer, the presence of the Holy Spirit, and for bold and gifted enthusiasts working together to grow the kingdom of God through the church.
>
> When the story is finished, you who listened within the number one, two, and three roles can share what resonates for you. Together, try to select the most dominant seasonal application for this particular story. Does it lie within the Christmas cycle, the Easter cycle, or the Pentecost cycle? Come to consensus if you can. If you cannot come to consensus, then let the original storyteller, number four, make the selection based on your discussion. When you have finished telling one story and agreed upon its location in the church year, move the numbers around and repeat the process until all four participants have played out all four of the roles.

I observed the groups' work with a great deal of interest. Most of the groups were able to connect all four of their stories to particular seasons in the church year and name the dominant expressions of God's presence. But then something interesting and confusing happened. The more they reflected, the more intertwined their conclusions became. They saw aspects of all of the seasons coming together in a particular story. What originally seemed like a neat way to sort out the story became complicated, blended, and more confusing. The longer they talked, the more they felt that they had failed the assignment, had not understood it, or were not smart enough to sort it out within a neat rational framework.

At first I reacted with the same confusion, until together we realized that we had been drawn into mystery, into the very nature of a triune God and the heart of the story of the church. When we look at the Trinity we see separate and distinct "persons," but they always point to one another rather than draw attention to themselves. The Father, Abba, points to Jesus and the Spirit. Consider the transfiguration of Jesus, where the Father says, "This is my Son, the Beloved; listen to him!" (Mark 9:7). And the dove of the Spirit descended to rest on Jesus as well. In a pre-Christian setting, God points to the Spirit by saying through the prophet Joel that in the last days God's spirit would be poured upon all flesh.

Jesus points to the Almighty One and tells parables to illustrate that God is like a loving Father, calling him "Abba." He prays to his Father in heaven. And he promises that the Spirit will come as a comforter who will baptize with fire. This same Spirit will continue to remind believers of all that Jesus had taught them.

The Spirit points to the Father by illuminating Scripture. The Spirit functions as divine spectacles through which we more clearly see the truth of the Word of God. And the Spirit points to Jesus at the table where bread is broken and wine poured out.

Each pointing to the other would ultimately be confusing if it were not for the relationship among the three. The loving and trusting relationship creates a wholeness and unity that defies reason but projects a picture of God. When we refer to one person of the Godhead, we really are speaking of all three. In their relationship, we see love perfectly expressed in giving, serving while yielding, and empowering while enthusing. When looking at the three members in the Trinity, we see the mystery expressed in a complete package of relationships.

Just as the persons of the Trinity point to each other in loving relationship, so do the stories of particular church seasons. A story that seems to be dominated by one season is drawn into relationship with other seasonal stories. When that happens, we might consider moving it into a new space in the seasonal motif. When we root our stories in trinitarian spirituality, we cannot allow those stories to be set in concrete but will allow those stories to be nudged and reframed for a new day and season.

TRINITARIAN SPIRITUAL FORMATION

My interest in trinitarian spiritual formation via storytelling and reflection has developed while engaging in various types of volunteer service and ministry. After my retirement as director of Worshipful-Work, my wife and I spent a year as volunteers at Sterling College in Sterling, Kansas. (Joyce rendered hospitality at the newly restored Old Main on campus, Cooper Hall. We had first met on the front steps of that grand old building fifty years earlier.) I volunteered in their servant leadership initiative, for which I had served as a consultant in their planning and exploration process. New awareness of servant qualities in the second person of the Trinity was taking shape on campus. A beautiful bronze statue of Peter kneeling to wash Jesus's feet graced the entrance to Cooper Hall, and students would pat Jesus on the shoulder as they walked by. But an interpretive and consciousness-raising task still needed to be accomplished with the total academic community. I was asked to lead morning and evening prayers centered on the book of Isaiah's servant passages during the Lenten season. We opened our eyes to the Trinity through the pictures of Jesus, Israel, and the church acting as servant.

During a daily chapel service, the chaplain, Henry Lederle, formerly from the Reformed Church in South Africa, offered a theological foundation for servant leadership. He took the text, "Every scribe who has been trained for the kingdom of heaven is like the master of a household who brings out of his treasure what is new and what is old" (Matt. 13:52). Lederle employed the Christian doctrine of the Trinity to illustrate both the old and the new. The old treasure looks to traditional orthodoxy, picturing God the Father as Creator, giving every individual worth and dignity. Jesus the Son gave his life to save the world. The Spirit offers comfort and power.

So what are the new treasures rooted in trinitarian spirituality? He went on to describe God the Father as a deeply relational person who enters into covenant with people, thereby inviting us into deeper personal relationships with one another and the created universe. The new treasure of the Son, a suffering servant, beckons us to join him in servant leadership via self-denial, sacrificial giving, and forfeiting the opportunity to take advantage of others. The new treasure from the Spirit calls us to a forward-looking, hope-filled life along with gifts for that future. Both the old and the new awareness of treasure can be embraced. If the community embraces both the old and the new, a new day will dawn. He summarized his rationale for rooting servant leadership in the Trinity:

> The old treasures I outlined first as being inclusive and more democratic, since all have been created equal in God's sight; secondly as learning to exhibit humility and service; and thirdly as recognizing everyone's gifts and strengths. These qualities are transforming leadership training in this nation and further abroad.
>
> The new treasures that Christians may discover in our storehouse are a deeper quality of personal relationships based on covenant; an attitude of sacrifice and self-denial based on the

cross; and a forward-looking, hopeful stance based on the resurrection and the Spirit as the foretaste and first installment of
the future. May these facets of truth renew us as we clasp the
treasure of that great idea—to become servant leaders.[1]

If the idea of servant leadership is only seen through the example
of Jesus, it will limit our spiritual growth and understanding. But
if it is tied to a larger awareness of God's presence through the
Trinity, we can allow servant leadership to blend and intertwine
our stories together into a powerful whole.

John Polkinghorne, noted theologian and physicist, shows
how new insights from quantum physics point to an underlying
trinitarian structure for the universe. He proposed an evidence-
based argument for the Trinity based on "evidence from below." I
would connect his reference to "evidence from below" to the stories of congregations in this book that have been associated with
the church year—lived out in worship and prayer to the Father,
through the Son, and in the power of the Spirit. Polkinghorne
observes:

> Trinitarian theologians have to hold on to their affirmation of
> the triune character of one true God, even if they cannot fully
> articulate an explanation of how this can be the case. . . . The
> threat of paradox cannot be dealt with simply by neglecting or
> denying the motivating experience. In holding on to a Trinitarian
> understanding of God, theologians can take heart from the fact
> that their belief receives some support from collateral consider-
> ation—i.e., as being in communion. . . . This insight certainly
> accords with an increasing scientific recognition of the relational
> character of the physical universe. The old-fashioned atomism
> that pictured isolated particles rattling around in the otherwise
> empty container of space has long been replaced by General
> Relativity's integrated account of space, time, and matter, under-
> stood to be combined in a single package deal. . . . The physical

world looks more and more like a universe that would be the fitting creation of the Trinitarian God, the One whose deepest reality is relational.

Finally, the picture of the three Persons, eternally united in the mutual exchange of love, gives a profound insight into the meaning of that foundational Christian conviction that "God is love."[2]

Trinitarian spiritually fosters the wholeness we seek as individuals. It becomes a model for personhood, what it means to be created in the image of God and to be fully human. Ego-centeredness and self-will never lead us down the path of wholeness. We find wholeness only in God.

My spiritual director, the late Father Joe Smerke of the Crosier Order, used to remind me that we are made in the image of God. Therefore, we (as well as the church) reflect the trinitarian nature of God. We are body, mind, and soul. He diagrammed the relationship with two triangles. (See fig. 7.1 and 7.2.)

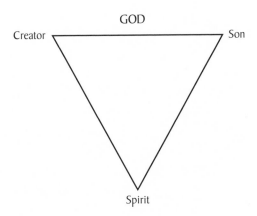

Figure 7.1. God may be depicted by a triangle.

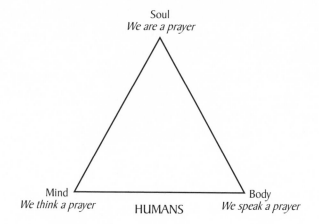

Figure 7.2. We humans may be depicted by an upright triangle.

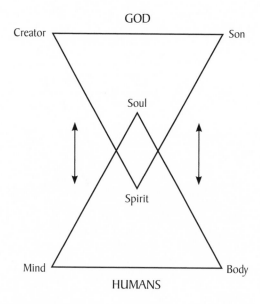

Figure 7.3. Triangles beginning to Intersect.

When we picture the two triangles in moving toward and intersecting with each other, the lines may cut through each other in sometimes difficult and painful ways (see fig. 7.3). We may be called upon to let go of our resistance to God's moving into our lives. The points of the triangle meet, penetrate one another, and the sides eventually become integrated through spiritual formation until we are left with a Star of David! This star depicts our union with God (fig. 7.4).

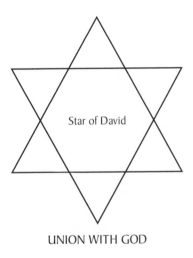

UNION WITH GOD

Figure 7.4. Union with God.

Trinitarian spirituality serves as a model for personal wholeness and also for corporate life. The mystery of the Trinity emphasizes community—a way of being together as the church. Father Joe's merging triangles could just as easily picture the triune God interacting with a group of people. Trinitarian spirituality lived out in the church can be seen in multiple healing and affirming relationships. So we should not wonder or be surprised when our stories relate to more than one of the seasons of the year or lead us to name several ways in which a trinitarian God is present. One season finds its fullest meaning in relationship to the other two, just as the persons of the Trinity do. After all, where you find one person of the Trinity, you find all three. This is mystery. They are always engaged together in the same single work!

Mystery is inherent in spiritual theology. We may not resolve seeming paradoxes into neat packages but we can offer them together in confession:

> In life and in death we belong to God.
> Through the grace of our Lord Jesus Christ,
>   The love of God,
>   And the communion of the Holy Spirit,
> We trust in the one triune God, the Holy One of Israel,
>   Whom alone we worship and serve.[3]

And we offer them in doxology:

> Praise God, from whom all blessings flow;
> Praise God, all creatures here below;
> Praise God above, all heavenly host;
> Praise Father, Son, and Holy Ghost!

Even though consideration of our stories will lead us to the church seasons, into a scriptural message behind the season, and finally into the mystery of trinitarian presence and theology, the process does not need to paralyze us or leave us spellbound. The very nature of the waltz of the gospel frees us and propels us into creating the next story on the journey of faith. We do not want to be stuck in the past or mesmerized by the present. We want to be able to move toward a new future. We start with the story. When we reflect on that story and recast it into a new one, we will discover that the story indeed becomes a song.

CHAPTER 8

When the Story
Becomes a Song

Stories often become treasures. We know this from personal experience. It is hard to imagine what we would bring to community life or important relationships were it not for the memories we hold dear. Our identity is rooted in the traditions of our ancestors, the settings in which we grow up, the events we experience, and choices we make across the years. We only really know who we are or where we are going in light of where we have been.

While story has value for individuals, it is of even greater importance for communities, especially communities of faith. Congregations have histories—story lines, ancient and recent—that are a treasure trove waiting to be mined for meaning, wisdom, and a way into the future. If we ignore them, life becomes diminished. We embrace them for the rich rewards they promise. Mining stories takes time and effort, requiring skilled leadership and determination to stick with the process until the jewel is cut and polished to reveal its ultimate value.

Unfortunately, congregational narratives are often ignored or become buried beneath the clutter of active programming and church busyness. For many congregational leaders and members, the narratives do not seem to hold enough practical value to warrant much attention. Their treasure is seldom recognized and is often ignored. Yet stories can become the source of valuable spiritual wisdom.

Many of us grew up singing the old gospel hymn "Blessed Assurance": "This is my story. This is my song: Praising my Savior all the day long." Followers of Billy Graham's evangelistic crusades remember those moments when the song leader, George Beverly Shea, brought the assembly's voices to a crescendo while he drew out the words "This . . . is . . . my . . ." before continuing, "story, this is my song." If the song has held so much emotional and spiritual punch for individuals, imagine what "This is *our* story, this is *our* song" could mean for congregations! Both communal stories and individual faith stories, upon which communal stories are constructed, can become songs.

How can the story become a song? When does that happen? I believe it happens when we name God's presence in the story. But if we ignore the story in the first place or fail to reflect on it along the way, we will find it difficult to celebrate God's powerful influence as a player in the story. Human experience provides a starting place for composing a song. Then the composer attaches a simple tune, expands that tune, creates a poetic version of the story, searches for feeling tones that will touch the heart, and finally rests with satisfaction in a work of art well done. In our own American music culture, country-and-western songs illustrate how this process takes place. Writers of these songs begin with life experience, search for deeper meanings by tapping into other sources of wisdom, and connect these to singable melodies. Then the new songs resonate with yearnings, aspirations, and hopes of others. The song becomes a powerful tool of communication and a source of celebration. People in congregations need to feel the beat, hear the tones, articulate the words of the story, connect the story with wisdom and tradition, and sing its culmination to God in praise and prayer.

Let's walk step by step through the developmental process from the story to a song. I will present eight steps in numerical order. If you are a trained musician, you can translate them into the seven notes on a C major scale, beginning with middle C—with the eighth note, C, completing the octave. If you are not a trained musician but are familiar with Julie Andrews's singing the "Do, Re, Mi" song in the movie *The Sound of Music,* you can hear the eight notes (do, re, mi, fa, sol, la, ti, and do) as a song that incorporates and completes the process of the story becoming a song. (This way of assigning syllables to names of the musical scale is called *solfege.* Syllable names originally came from a well-known medieval hymn, *Ut queant laxis,* a hymn to St. John the Baptist, in which each successive stanza starts on the next higher note.)

STEP I: SEE THE VALUE OF STORYTELLING

A potential treasure is mined for its meaning within the faith community because its value is appreciated. Elaborate mining operations are only put into place because the potential value of the ore has been predetermined. Sometimes a group of church leaders— members of the church board or council—show little interest in telling stories because they think they are the sole property of the clergy for sermon illustrations to communicate a point. Or they relegate storytelling to the church school classroom, believing the goal of storytelling is to bring the ancient tradition into a current awareness. They rarely focus on their own communal stories as a board, however, thinking that their more important task is to do "church business." Moderators of meetings rarely place corporate storytelling on meeting agendas because it is seen as having little value. Church boards tend to rely more on business plans, numerical goals, and program planning, which are more manageable but often lack soul, a lively spirit.

Some board leaders do allow for stories about the "good old days," but telling those stories often makes at least some of the people around the board table feel left out. The person who reminisces might value storytelling a lot—as long as he or she gets to tell his or her story. Some boards have been burned by a storyteller who drones on, boring the group with too many self-congratulating references. In spite of bad experiences with storytelling, some members might value stories in general but not this particular story, which they do not feel a part of or are tired of hearing. "That was in the past, and we were not there. So what's the use or the point?" They may fear that by giving too much attention to a story about the good old days, the board will get stuck in the past when it really needs to move on to a preferred future.

If the story to be mined involves past conflicts, church leaders may tacitly agree to keep silent out of fear that they will be pulled back into the conflict and will not be able to handle its heat. One interim pastor did not serve the congregation very well when he refused to allow the church board to form a common story around the previous pastor's leaving. The subject festered for several months into the new, settled pastor's ministry until he invited board members to share their perceptions of the story. Only then did the board discover that no dark secrets had forced the former pastor to leave. Having finally told their story together, the tension evaporated, and they moved on.

A leadership team may be so enamored with anything new—innovative, clever, faddish—that they think they have no time for what seems old and familiar. They always focus on the future and become so preoccupied with what lies in front of them that they are unwilling to consider their common stories. They often assume that everyone already knows the stories and think, why rehash something old and of no current value? Beyond that, they may devalue the story-mining process because they think they do not have the skills to discern God's presence in the story, which translates it into a song.

Some years ago I listened to Martin E. Marty, noted contemporary church historian, deliver a lecture to a group of students at Columbia Theological Seminary in Decatur, Georgia. During the question-and-answer session that followed, one of the students asked Dr. Marty, "How can you pass yourself off as a 'contemporary church historian'? Aren't you so much in the middle of the story that your perspective may be easily tainted by the culture around you?" Dr. Marty responded, "You have to trust and check reliable sources. I have two that I rely upon. The first is automobile bumper stickers. If a person feels strongly enough about a matter to place a sticker on the back bumper of the car for all to see and reap the harvest of comments about it, he or she tells it like it is. The other is a campfire setting when men are away from home with a beer or two in their bellies. They tell life like it is for them." Leaders are surrounded with important stories with which they can work. They can trust that a process that helps them examine and reflect theologically on those stories will be a productive one.

Church leaders—especially church boards—should see themselves as stewards of the stories of their congregations. As such, they can prompt new stories to be told, allow them to form in corporate memory, reflect on their meaning and significance, and include them in ritual celebrations. If they do not see any value in working with their stories, they will not allow them to come up in the first place.

Old mining towns may still be found in many mountainous regions of the West. At one time, thousands of people lived in those towns and worked the mines. Folks rushed to the West with gold fever, because gold was held in high value. Later, many of those mines shut down, creating ghost towns, not necessarily because they ran out of ore, but because they determined that the low value of the ore would not make mining it profitable. Stories are like precious metal. When their own bearers value them highly, they can produce a rich reward for those who will extend the effort to mine them for newfound wisdom. Without mining their stories, congregations can become hollow spiritual and theological ghost towns.

STEP 2: TAKE TIME TO TELL STORIES

For a story to ultimately become a song, it must first be allowed to have a life of its own. It needs space to thicken, deepen, and

unfold. This happens when a group adopts the practice of forming corporate memory around its stories. The narratives may be
drawn from a thin, recent slice of memory or from an elongated
slab over a period of several years. Sadly, this practice of forming
corporate memory is rarely pursued in a timely way. Folks assume everyone knows the stories, or they are tucked away in the
folder of the church historian, or they surface in smaller group-
ings around coffee tables and in church parking lots. If corporate
stories are not birthed in the leadership circles of the church, an
impression soon arises among leaders and members that nothing
significant happens in the congregation. It will find itself without
a song and no sense of movement on a journey.

A group of pastors and lay leaders from United Methodist
churches in western Kansas gathered for a day of church board
development. I scouted for a team from one church that could
come up front to tell the whole group a story from their congregational life. During the coffee break, I approached five members
from a particular church and invited them to do that. They responded to a person, "Nothing's happened in our church—not
this past year or in the past three or in the past five years. We did
get rid of a pastor, but we don't want to tell that story." Failing to
enlist them, I went on my way. Later during that break, three of
those five individuals came to me separately and told me what
happened in church the previous Sunday! So when the group re-
convened, I invited the five them to come forward and tell their
story of what happened in church last Sunday. They related that
eight new members had joined the church. Two of them, adults,
were baptized. Most could not remember a time when an adult
had joined the church by profession of faith. They told the story
of their church—its history, their town, the hope a new pastor
instilled, the past resistance by those families who joined to invest
in the church, and so on. It took them a good thirty minutes to get
out the story about what had happened last Sunday. Yet these were
the very same people who were not aware that they had a story to

tell. Why not? Because before our training session, no corporate memory had been formed among them, recited, ritualized, or celebrated. Conversations about that Sunday morning service had probably been told in cars on the way home from church, around family lunch tables, or in casual conversations between members in their comings and goings—but not around their council table. Corporate memory had not been formed at the leadership heart of the church. The process that could have led to celebration in song never commenced.

In an earlier chapter, I mentioned a church in which a congregation voted by a narrow margin to reject the nomination of a pastor's spouse to an associate pastoral position, leaving most everyone up in the air or with bruised feelings. I asked a leader of that church if their church council could have told that story at its next council meeting. He replied, "Yes, but only if we were accustomed to forming corporate memory around our stories as a month-by-month practice." Because they had not engaged in storytelling about the small and ordinary aspects of their life, they were not prepared to take on emotionally charged stories. They kept the stories under the table and defaulted into a conspiracy of silence.

Over the years the Worshipful-Work model got great mileage out of a simple little device that can be used to prompt corporate stories. I call it "and then . . . but before that . . ." In a group, a facilitator helps the group identify a starting place for the story. Participants are then invited to spontaneously provide the next brief part of the story, introducing it with "and then . . ." or "but before that . . ." The second lead, "but before that," usually relieves tension and often provides a note of humor. This has become an official part of the framework I as a facilitator offer to folks to help them get started with a story and form corporate memory around it. When my Texas friends use this technique, they say, "But there is a third lead: 'Meanwhile, back at the ranch!' To understand this story, you need some background." At times this may be appropriate, but I ask them to hold off for the time being, not to interpret the story prematurely. They are simply to get the story out together. I urge them to hold any interpretations or special spins for the reflection process, which will come later.

In facilitating corporate memory formation with church groups, I am regularly impressed with the depth of the communal stories they tell. The stories are so much fuller and more alive than when they come from a single storyteller's experience and observations. This particular method or practice of forming corporate memory has proven so successful that I now commend its use in every board meeting, inviting the leaders of the meeting to schedule it into the agenda. I urge them to tell the story of one significant event that has happened in the congregation since their last meeting. As a result of regularly engaging in this practice, church leaders are better prepared to deal with uncomfortable and conflict-ridden stories. Furthermore, they come to a unified view of what the story actually is, which helps them make decisions later in the meeting that may relate to the story.

Some members around the table may decline to participate in forming a communal story, saying that they were not present or their impressions are only secondhand. But even secondhand information becomes reality, for it is actually part of the lore of the congregation with an energy of its own. If these people will contribute even hearsay "and then" or "before that" material, their input will help form a whole and thick story, which eventually self-corrects. That is one of the reasons I encourage everyone to use first-person plural (we) pronouns rather than first-person singular (I) pronouns while telling the story. Then they all can own the whole story.

The events around which corporate memory forms may include the entire history of the church from its founding and across the years. In that event an extended retreat or special meeting will allow sufficient time to form and work with the story. This is especially profitable for members who have just joined the group.

When they look together at the long history of the church, they will recognize patterns that give clues to the church's particular spiritual DNA. Or a story may be drawn from a shorter era of the congregation's life, such as a particular decade, a pastor's tenure, or an extended project. It could also be about a single, brief event.

One vestry formed corporate memory by telling their story of the annual breakfast they served to the parish—including their embarrassment of forgetting to bring and serve orange juice. They were able to come up with a suitable substitute, so when they later processed their story, Jesus's miracle of turning water into wine at a marriage feast came to mind.

Another church council came to their annual retreat on a Saturday morning with fresh memories and wounds from a contentious congregational meeting that had been held the previous Sunday. A few loud and disgruntled members had attacked the pastor, council, and members of the church. The retreat leader laid aside her plan for the retreat and invited them to tell the story of the congregational meeting, using "and then . . . but before that." They took an hour and a half to tell the story. Then she suggested that they break for a half hour of silence during which they could go for a walk and look for an item to bring back to the group as a symbol of hope. When the group reassembled, each person showed the item they had chosen and explained how it expressed their hope. Through their sharing, a new tenderness, support, and understanding graced the gathering. Their memories of those strident voices from the prior Sunday were tempered and appreciated in a different way.

My friend Peter Morgan, former director of the Disciples of Christ Historical Society, says to congregations about to tell a corporate story, "Get the story. Get it straight. And get it out." We may tend to run from the most difficult aspects of a story, but real stories are those that come from the gut. Owning and working with them will put us on a path to authentic spirituality. Corporate memories, conceived in gracious space, can become the grist for spiritual development and offer important notes for the song we yearn to sing.

STEP 3: NURTURE THE STORY

If the opening notes that emerge from shared stories are not allowed to more fully develop in the heart and mind of a composer, the potential song will die a premature death. How tragic! Folks who experience a sudden change in fortune grieve the loss, not simply for what is but also for what might have been. The same tragic circumstance may occur when a tune lies dormant. What might it have become? When church leaders birth a story but then lay it aside, not nurturing it, feeding it, or developing it into a thick, powerful resource for self-understanding and eventual celebration, it will never become a song.

Various methods can be used to deepen and expand a story. Asking questions about the story may further develop it:

> Where does this story fit in the long history of our congregation?
> Are any seeds of this story embedded in our founding story?
> Does this story reflect any recurring themes in the longer story?
> Who were the players in the story, and what were their roles?
> If we were selecting a symbol for the story, what would it be?
> What was happening in the culture outside the church at this time?
> Who were the wisdom bearers in the story?
> Is any important information missing from the story we have told?

A longer congregational story may be created by laying a printed timeline over several tables or posting it on a wall and then inviting participants to write their own memories and impressions of church events below the line. Then I ask church councils to record above the line events that happened in the wider culture.

They list events such as wars, floods, fires, droughts, accidents, elections, and so forth. Ronald Reagan's name appeared on one congregation's timeline. When I asked the leaders of this inner city congregation why his name was included, they responded that during the Reagan administration, a number of community programs were curtailed, leaving the church to take up the slack and to care for poor people in their neighborhood.

The timeline is one helpful tool. A number of other tools are available for use by leadership groups to enlarge the stories with which they are working. More than a decade ago, James P. Wind, now president of the Alban Institute, wrote a workbook called *Constructing Your Congregation's Story*. Now out of print, the workbook has been adapted for posting on the Alban Institute website. The following description of his work by an Alban resource team member offers clues to the effective development of a story:

> Because there is much to be done when constructing a congregational history, Wind emphasizes that a community needs to be engaged in the effort. This community may begin by exploring the congregation's raw materials and documents. But it will also need to involve the whole congregation in the discovery process, ensuring a safe place for people to honestly tell their stories.
>
> The author explains some valuable skills for researchers: an intense curiosity, a healthy skepticism, a creative imagination, and a solid filing system. He encourages researchers to approach their congregations from the perspective of an outsider—by looking with fresh eyes at a congregation's building, neighborhood, liturgical symbols, organizations, activities, official and unofficial leaders, and significant transitions. He also encourages researchers to explore how the pastor and people embody their faith in the world. Wind concludes with instruction on how to tell a story that is truthful and fair, whole, human, and interesting—one that speaks to present and future audiences.[1]

A helpful technique for telling a story about a specific incident is to ask, "Is anything missing in this story?" Often an extended silence follows the question until someone breaks the silence with a statement that opens the floodgates for a rush of additional information. That is when we hear, "then our pastor left . . . then a lot of people left the church . . . then our pastor was accidentally killed . . . we disagreed about the matter . . . a child spoke wisdom to us . . . a little thing made a big difference."

The session and deacons of Northminster Presbyterian Church of Indianapolis gathered for a daylong retreat toward the end of an extended interim ministry. I invited them to tell the congregation's story during the 1990s using the "and then . . . but before that . . ." method. Their story unfolded in a comfortable fashion until they came to an extended pause, finally interrupted by someone who said, "I might as well say it, because everyone knows it. Our pastor and his wife were murdered in their home in Advent of that year." Yes, everyone in the room knew of the incident, but they had not all been aware of vital information around the fringes of the story. As the story spilled out, the group heard about the role of the session, the role of the police, how and where communication took place, and the fact that in the subsequent two years the stream of visitors they had always enjoyed had been nearly shut off. This large, prominent church was accustomed to the presence of visitors, but after the murders, the surrounding community did not know how to relate to the congregation. As the story was updated, participants heard information that the children of the church had recently made thousands of cards inviting the congregation's neighbors to visit the church, and those cards had just been mailed. By telling this whole story, participants were further developing their corporate memory. The board of the church embraced a very painful story, not yielding to the temptation to keep it a secret. Working with the whole story brought some degree of healing and freed them to move into a new significant pastoral relationship and ministry. Incidentally, when I preached in worship the following Sunday morning, a number of visitors were present. They had accepted the invitation of the children. It was a sign. The fullness of the story added notes to the potential new song.

STEP 4: CONNECT THE STORY TO SCRIPTURE AND TRADITION

The next critical step in the story's movement toward becoming a song has to do with its connection to tradition, a bridge we can make by asking, What time is it? Or, Where does our story fit within the seasons of the church year? The church year provides a way for us to enter into the tradition of Scripture. We see new light on the path to God's Word, which illuminates the story. If we intertwine our stories with the biblical tradition, we can then reflect theologically on their meaning. We see them in relationship to each other, which prompts deeper questions and fosters new affirmations of faith and hope. Peter Morgan, whom I mentioned above, calls this process "story weaving," in which woof and warp interact to produce a beautiful fabric. Stories for the warp come from the Bible and tradition. Stories for the woof come from life in the congregation.[2] If we do not explore our unfolding story in light of Scripture, the resulting fabric will be bland and the potential song will be muted.

Unfortunately, lay leaders who lack confidence about their grasp of Scripture may decline to do biblical and theological reflection, saying, "We don't know enough about the Bible to do it. Let the professionals have it." Even when scripture texts are included in the devotional portion of a committee meeting, members may not make immediate connections between those texts and matters on the agenda of the meeting. Arnold Smit, a consultant and trainer from South Africa, researched the interaction of spiritual practice with church governance for a doctoral project. He and his team visited forty-four church committee meetings. All of the meetings opened with prayer. Many of them included various types of opening devotions. A few included intensive Bible study. In their evaluation, they discovered that most participants liked opening prayer. Fewer liked opening devotions. And hardly anyone liked intensive Bible study. "Why not?" they were asked. Their answer: "Because it takes too much time away from doing business." As the researchers observed the remainder of the meetings, they noted the complete absence of any reference to the scriptural passages heard during the opening part of the meeting. No stories, themes, or people were mentioned. The committees offered no prayers about the decisions they were trying to make. They never framed their discussions around questions such as, What is God calling us to do? Where is God leading us? What is God's will for us in the matter? Smit concluded that two separate and distinct cultures operated at the committee table. One was a culture of religious practice. The other was a culture of parliamentary procedure and organizational science. One book was opened to begin the meeting. Then it was closed and a second was opened.

What is an antidote to this separation? How can story and Scripture be interwoven? While working with the story, ask what season of the church year most closely matches this congregational story. Can it be found in the Advent and Christmas cycle, in the Lenten and Easter cycle, or in the Pentecost cycle? What waiting and yearning reside within the story: hope, anxiety, or centered prayer? Does the story reflect the love of God or the grace of Jesus or the power of the Spirit? What invitations to proclaim and send forth workers flow from the story? Does the story most closely match Epiphany light, or Eastertide life, or the greening and growing of the kingdom in Pentecost?

Here is a variation of the traditional timeline. Take another look at the bell curve graph in chapter 2 (fig. 2.2), which identifies the rhythmic triads of the seasons of the church year. Place that diagram on a table or wall, label the seasons, and invite participants to place the stories of the congregation in corresponding seasons. Plot your communal stories on that bell curve map, which outlines the nine movements in the season of the church year. Where would you place them? Once the seasons for your stories have been located, ask yourself, What biblical stories come to mind when I or we think of those particular seasons? The character of the stories will dictate where they match the biblically informed church seasons. When local stories and traditional wisdom of the seasons match, a tune for your song is being created.

STEP 5: CLARIFY UNDERLYING MEANING, VALUE, AND BELIEF

Biblical and theological reflection upon our stories takes us further down the path toward realization of a song. We are able to isolate meanings and values from allowing each scripture and each story to speak to the other. These values can then be applied to life and ministry. We are able to make belief statements and affirmations of faith that spring from our own lived experience. The reflection process, however, invites far more than a values clarification exercise. I will often ask storytelling and reflection groups to name what tenet they understand in a new way, what wisdom has been distilled, or what they believe they would now be willing to risk or to stake even their life on in order to be faithful. They may also want to connect their contemporary statements of belief to the creeds of their church.

Many church leadership groups face the task of writing a church's mission or purpose statement. Meaningful mission and purpose statements do not arise simply from a rational exercise. They must be solidly rooted in the real-life experience of faith, hope, and love as the congregation lives it out its day-to-day journey of faith. Values and beliefs that have surfaced from the congregation's practice of biblical and theological reflection on its own stories will produce a basis for their new statements.

Sometimes, however, words may fail, and we cannot put our beliefs into neat paragraphs. One church leadership group gave up on writing and instead selected a visual image. They chose a wellspring. Then they invited the congregation to see itself as a wellspring of living water to one another and to the community around the church. They urged every organization in the church to examine its own internal life and outreach by comparing it to a wellspring. To their surprise, they discovered that ministries took on new vitality within this visual purpose statement.

The Worshipful-Work model that I used with congregational boards over a number of years was constructed on four practices for board meetings. Those practices are (1) history giving and storytelling, (2) biblical and theological reflection, (3) envisioning the future, and (4) spiritual discernment.[3] Over time, as I trained leaders in using the model, more interest centered on discernment—making group decisions by coming to the mind of Christ in substance or in spirit. In this process, after the group selects and frames an issue for discernment, it is set before a decision-making group to seek God's will or yearning in the matter. Early in the discernment process, participants are asked to isolate guiding principles that will inform their exploration. Those guiding principles are to be closely tied to the whole of biblical wisdom rather than used as a proof text from a particular reference. If participants can agree on the guiding principles, then they will move rather quickly to a unified conclusion of the discernment. Also, if they sputter and bog down toward the end of the discernment process, they can revisit the guiding principles to see if the principles are clear and agreed upon.[4]

The locations for spiritual discernment may move beyond local church board tables to the assembly halls of denominations. When I was a guest in the home of Michael Thawley, former moderator of the Presbyterian Church of New Zealand, he reflected in an informal conversation on the difficulty his denomination had making controversial decisions. When members divided over issues, the sides seemed to follow two different guiding principles. Both can be found in the Bible, especially in the Old Testament.

Michael observed that one guiding principle reflected the values of holiness and purity. The other reflected the call for justice. He wondered how the people of Israel lived with these two principles side by side and if the principles even coexisted. If so, could the adherents of each side actually bless one other? He took his question to Walter Brueggemann, noted Old Testament scholar from Columbia Seminary, who pointed to the framers of the canon of Scripture. They included both the justice and holiness streams in the Old Testament canon, thereby allowing them to bless each other. That seeming contradiction suggests that we commit ourselves to more intentional listening, searching, and discerning of God's will in our own time. If, when we are making a decision, we can clarify the underlying guiding principles, we will save ourselves much time and effort. We can note whether the agreement is supported by uniform guiding principles or that a divided conclusion is rooted in contrasting guiding principles.

The popularity of Rick Warren's purpose-oriented material, generated from the Saddleback Church in Lake Forest, California, testifies to the value of an agreed-upon purpose. Efforts to come to agreement about vision, purpose, and mission will lead to a more harmonious conclusion. Conflicting or unclear purposes will diminish the potential beauty of the song we yearn to sing.

STEP 6: NOTICE AND NAME
HOW GOD IS PRESENT IN THE STORY

The process of working with our stories in order for them to become songs will require us to tell a complete story. The story will include spaces for us to allow for mystery, awe, and wonder—just as a good melody incorporates rests, which in turn accent the rhythms. Often we tend to push stories to predetermined conclusions to prove or illustrate a point, thereby preventing the story from fully developing and shortchanging its unfolding possibilities. When we use stories only to prove a line of thinking, we may leave God out of the story. When we allow silence, even awkward silence in a story, the Spirit has room to point to signs of God's presence in the ordinary activities of life. When we ask, What are the signs of God's presence here? we pause to taste and see that the Lord is good.

Church leaders often think they have to bring God into a situation, that this is their mission to a world without God. That may be a bit presumptuous. Roman Catholic theologian Robert J. Schreiter writes from his own experience in developing countries, especially Latin America. He suggests that all theologies are local—that is, that they arise out of the immediate experience of a faith community within a particular culture and setting. He suggests that Christians should compare their local theology with other local theologies expressed throughout the history of the church and in other cultures, placing church tradition—a series of local theologies—alongside local culture. He recommends first listening to the culture and making that culture, and God's presence in it, the starting point for the missionary enterprise.

> Beneath this approach for understanding—listening, developing a thick description, linking the balance between respect of the culture and the need for change within culture—lies a theological position that can be stated thus: the development of local theologies depends as much on finding Christ already active in the culture. The great respect for culture has a Christological basis. It grows out of a belief that the risen Christ's salvific activity in bringing about the kingdom of God is already going on before our arrival.[5]

What if church boards assumed that Christ was already a player in each story? What a difference that would make in moving the story toward a song! The story becomes song when that presence is noticed, named, and celebrated.

Many of the hymns we sing in church offer models for naming God's presence. The traditional hymn "Come Thou Fount of Every Blessing" contains a rather curious line in the second verse: "Here I raise my Ebenezer: 'Hither by Thy help I've come.'" The hymn refers to incidents in the history of Israel. The Ebenezer, meaning "stone of help," was a memorial signifying God's real presence in aiding God's people. Samuel set up a memorial stone and called it Ebenezer after prevailing against the Philistines in battle. He said, "Thus far the LORD has helped us" (1 Sam. 7:12). Building stone memorials of God's help was a common practice in ancient Israel. After crossing the Jordan River into the Promised Land, the Israelites gathered twelve stones from the riverbed and built a testimonial. While positioning their stones for the memorial, they verbally testified to how God helped them on their journey from Egypt to the Promised Land. When their children in later generations would see the pile of stones and ask about their meaning, they were to be told how God helped them cross over the Jordan in this very location (Josh. 4:1–7).

Church stories need Ebenezer-type spaces in them that can be filled with testimonies of God's special presence and help in times of need. With a sharpened sensitivity to the seasons of the church year, we can more easily relate the season of our story to the scripture and the seasonal rhythms of the church year. We will have noticed and can affirm the love of God, the grace of Jesus, and the power of the Spirit.

STEP 7: CELEBRATE GOD'S PRESENCE

In the ministry of Worshipful-Work, we trainers attempted to encourage integrating spirituality and administration at the boardroom table. One popular training workshop theme became, "The table of the board as a table of the Lord." Following one weekend seminar, a participant handed us a drawing that captured this theme. It showed a round board-type table with the top of a communion table superimposed on it at a ninety-degree angle, with two outstretched hands offering a broken loaf of bread. (See fig. 8.1.)

Fig. 8.1. The Table of the Board as a Table of the Lord[6]

Within church board agendas, devotions are usually placed at the front end of meetings for centering purposes. But we often recommended a variation: Place worship at the end of the meeting in order to offer to God "the stuff" of the meeting. I recall one board meeting where certain participants were asked at the outset to listen closely and make notes—one to gather reasons to give thanks, another to listen for matters that could be raised in intercessions, and another to notice evidence of God's presence either within the meeting itself or in the life of the church. They listened closely to the stories that were told and deliberations that ensued at the board table. At the close of the meeting, each designated person offered a prayer from the notes they had taken.

In other board meetings, participants opened their hymnals to suggest particular hymns that matched what God was doing in their midst, or they read prayers imbedded in Scripture with the name of their church inserted, or they attached their name or situation to the reading of Psalm 23.

If we name God's presence only through stale, dull, propositions, the possibility of the story becoming a song is dampened. But if our own story ends in doxology with praise and thanks to God, it has life and vitality. Specific stories of journey can lead to expressions of worship. They always carry more energy and excitement.

In the sacrament of the Lord's Supper, liturgical emphasis is increasingly being placed on the great prayer of thanksgiving, a recounting of God's acts of creation and redemption. Not only are thanks offered for the blessings of life, but the prayers also include the offering of our own brokenness and pain. When we offer our real, gut-wrenching experiences to God with thanksgiving, a miracle happens. We find healing and courage to go on. Christ is truly present with us. So it is no accident that many church boards celebrate the Lord's Supper at their own table as a way to offer their stories to God. Celebrating God's presence in a story converts the story into a song.

When we celebrate God's presence in our stories, we make a powerful witness to the world. Outsiders and visitors recognize it and are attracted to that kind of living church. If we do not name and celebrate God's presence in our common life and worship, they see a dull, lifeless, and hopeless church. Many churches look for effective evangelism programs that can help them appeal to outsiders. But what if telling church stories, matching them with the church seasons, and finally lifting them as offerings in song were seen as an evangelism tool itself? What a glorious day that would be! *This is our story. This is our song!"*

STEP 8: ENGAGE IN MISSION

Engaging in mission naturally follows celebrating God's presence in story reflection. Engagement in mission brings us to the possibility of a new story, so the process becomes circular. The seven steps we have taken with our stories do not lead us back to where we started but move us forward into a new story that we can process in the same manner. If you have attached a musical scale to these seven steps, you will recognize that the eighth note is the same as the first—but an octave apart. They resonate with one another in a consistent and complementary way.

The first step placed a high value on stories and led to the importance of beginning to tell the story. Having come to the eighth step, or in full circle on the music scale, we are now positioned for another story. So story begets story begets story. The ongoing process continues to multiply the number of songs in our collective repertoire. Just as pilgrims sang psalms of ascent on their way up to Jerusalem, we sing our way forward on the journey of faith, confident of the triune God's presence along the way.

APPENDIX A

How to Use This Book

FOR PERSONAL DEVOTIONS

Below are suggestions for using this book in morning and evening devotions.

In the Morning

- Read the section on morning prayer from Hours of the Day in chapter 2.
- Claim Psalm 5 to begin a new day.
- Read or sing one morning hymn from a hymnbook.
- Use the prayer example from the section "Kneeling" in chapter 1 as a way to join God's work for the day.

In the Evening or Night

- Follow the *examen*, described in chapter 1, to determine what you need to let go of before retiring. Read the section on night prayer in chapter 2.
- Open a hymnbook and look for the evening hymns. Read or sing one of the hymns daily each week.
- Claim Psalm 4 before resting in the night.
- Practice a method of prayer described in chapter 1, "Breathing."

AS A GUIDE IN KEEPING A JOURNAL

Here are a few ideas for creating a story journal:

- Create a symbol for each seasonal triad (total of nine) from chapters 2 and 3. Note figure 3.1, "The Waltz of the Gospel in Stories," in chapter 3.
- Then attach a symbol in the margin of the stories you record in your personal journal to identify the season of a particular story. You may do that as you write, or periodically go back to reread your journal, adding the symbols as you go.
- Read the account of Jim Thompson's faith sharing groups in chapter 2. Then pick out one significant story in your journal from the last year and place it in its congruent season.

IN A SIX-WEEK STUDY GROUP— ADVENT, LENT, OR THE GREAT FIFTY DAYS

Churches often look for resources to use in a four-to six-week span for small support groups or Sunday morning elective courses. The Advent, Lent, and Fifty Days periods offer a unique opportunity for participants to go deep into understanding and practicing spiritual formation.

Introduce the series by reading the preface and introduction, and "In the Seasons of the Church Year" from the last part of chapter 2. Then dwell on the chart "The Waltz of the Gospel in Stories" from chapter 3, inviting participants to select the season of the year with which they are most familiar or unfamiliar. Finally, allow the chapter 3 content to draw them deeply into the spiritual dynamics of each of the nine dance steps of the gospel.

From chapter 8, look at step 2, "Take Time to Tell Stories," to begin to formulate group stories from your congregational life.

Then connect them to the church year, look at the biblical content behind them, and celebrate God's presence in them.

TO TEACH A CONFIRMATION CLASS

Young people in particular enjoy reflecting on practical experience. Portions of this book can be adapted for use in a confirmation class. Introduce the three movements of letting go, naming God's presence, and taking hold from the introduction. Then structure all of the content input and experiential opportunities around those three repeating themes. Select specific practices from chapter 1 for them to consider and experience together, tying them to the threefold eternal rhythm. Help them see those in the various time frames presented in chapter 2.

Help them into the practice of journaling to form their own stories, then connect those stories to the seasons of the year.

If the class runs the greater part of a year, pick and choose from chapter 3, "The Waltz of the Gospel," to introduce and help them live into each season on a calendar basis. You might ask them to participate in planning and conducting weekly worship and to add what they have learned from their experience each week so that it becomes a discovery process.

TO WRITE A CHURCH HISTORY

Often the history of a church is framed around the tenure of its particular pastors or when buildings were built, burned, flooded, or torn down. What if the history was organized and grouped around the dynamics of the seasons of the church year rather than the chronology of decades and centuries?

Create an opportunity for people to tell and relate their own personal stories, then attach them to the larger story structured around the church year. Use the graph of the rhythmic triads of the church year from chapter 2.

TO PLAN A MAJOR
CHURCH ANNIVERSARY CELEBRATION

As part of a church anniversary celebration, introduce the seasons of the church year to a large, gathered assembly, using material from the introduction, the last section of chapter 2, and all of chapter 3. Invite each person to outline and date a corporate story of the congregation at large, plus a personal story. Ask them to mark a season for each.

Arrange the large room with six or nine "story centers" based on the nine steps in the waltz of the gospel, with a facilitator at each table or room location.

On cue, have people first bring a personal story to the matching location and share it with others who have assembled there. When that has run its course, invite them to move to a table or area where they can participate in telling a corporate story that relates to one of the waltz steps. In each one, have the listeners name their sense of God's presence.

Finally, as all reassemble for closing worship, invite affirmations of belief, naming of God's presence, and celebration of a trinitarian God.

TO TRAIN NEW CHURCH
OFFICERS AND LEADERSHIP TEAMS

Training leaders in an approach to congregational stories and the wisdom of church seasons is important. Effective lay leaders will need to know and operate out of the same church story. Create a timeline to visually see the unfolding life of the church, with opportunities for each person to add notes of personal association. After the timeline has been completed, invite the participants to place symbols of the nine dance steps around each entry. The bell curve diagram from chapter 2 offers an alternate way to connect stories to the church seasons.

Introduce the importance of using stories in deliberative meetings. Walk leaders through the eight steps in chapter 8 and practice the steps with specific communal stories.

TO PLAN SERMONS FOR THE YEAR

Begin sermon planning by consulting the recommended lectionary readings for each Sunday of the year. After seeing the framework of the eternal rhythm that is presented in this book's introduction, apply it to the Scriptures, personal stories, and real stories in the congregation. Instead of using stories to illustrate or prove an existing point, start with the story and then model the movement from the story to the song. Follow the sequence from chapter 8.

TO OPEN CHURCH BOARD
AND COMMITTEE MEETINGS

At the beginning of every board meeting, use the "and then . . . but before that" method of forming corporate memory around a story that has happened in the church since the last meeting. Then reflect biblically and theologically on that story and name signs of God's presence in it. Move through the steps in chapter 8.

Over a period of six meetings, look at a specific story in each meeting from the churches named Trinity in chapters 4, 5, and 6. In discussions, ask members what surprised them in the story and what the story invites them to consider for their congregation's vision or mission.

TO USE AS A GUIDE FOR THE
ANNUAL MEETING OF A CONGREGATION

For the congregation's annual meeting, select one to three important stories from the past year and invite the whole assembled group to tell each story in sequence using the "and then . . . but before that" method of forming corporate memory, which is presented in chapter eight. After each story invite members to place the story into one of the seasons of the church year (nine steps of the waltz or six major seasons). Use the story and reflections to lift the life of the church before God in thanksgiving, lament, intercession, or praise.

In addition or as an alternative, place members in groups of four and use the method of story sharing and reflection presented in chapter 7.

TO RECORD THE MINUTES OF A MEETING

The recording secretary of a deliberative meeting could write the minutes up as a communal spiritual journal rather than just a record of decisions made. Each reference that contains a story could be included and identified with a season of the church year. Or stories, ideas, and reflections could be grouped together and written accordingly. God's presence can be named as can evidences of letting go and taking hold.

TO READ AND DISCUSS
IN A BOOK GROUP

Form a group to read and discuss the contents of the book on a week-by-week and chapter-by-chapter basis. Allow the discussion to include personal or communal stories with the presentations.

TO USE WITH
ANOTHER BOOK OR A MOVIE

Any book or artistic presentation of the presence of God in human experience would fit nicely in dialogue with this book. For instance, the Presbyterian Church (U.S.A.) study document,

"The Trinity: God's Love Overflowing," would add a theological statement to our experiential component. William Paul Young's best-selling novel *The Shack,* in which a person with a painful life experience encounters a trinitarian God, could be placed alongside this book for a deepening understanding of God via the seasons of the church year. A group would have fun with the international award-winning movie *Babette's Feast* by seeing it through the waltz of the gospel.

After reading this book, a group might want to see a movie together or associate their own favorite books, movies, art, or statements of belief to the eternal rhythms of spiritual formation presented here.

TO BUILD AN EBENEZER

Find a desirable place in the church yard on which to erect a memorial stone monument testifying to the ways "God has helped us" along the journey (chapter 8). Ask each person, family, or group in the church to bring a stone to the church on the appointed day for constructing the Ebenezer. The Ebenezer may be built as a permanent memorial with stone and mortar or laid as a temporary pile of rocks without mortar. Invite each person, family, or group to give testimony to how God helps (or helped) them as their stone is put in place. Later, when they show the Ebenezer to inquiring visitors, they can point to their particular stone and tell why they put it there. In so doing, they will continue to recite the way God's presence has been named and celebrated on their journey.

Giving Testimony

From 1992 to 1994, the Reverend Jim Thompson conducted a series of small group sessions at Westminster Presbyterian Church in Des Moines, Iowa, in relation to his Doctor of Ministry project with Sioux Falls Seminary in Sioux Falls, South Dakota. He explored how associating the participants' own faith stories with the seasons of the church year could be formative in their spiritual growth. Jim told me about his work in a personal conversation prior to his unexpected death due to a brain tumor and encouraged me to look at his research. See chapter 2 for details. The following testimonies are drawn from participants in his groups and are a tribute to his life and ministry.

ADVENT SEASON

It is good to think of advent as it applies to our lives in an ongoing manner. I would hate to live without waiting in a spirit of anticipation. After reading advent Scripture I have two thoughts: (1) We don't always freely appreciate or understand what God has in store for us. Mary and Elizabeth had to wonder if God was playing games with them or whether things would work out. (2) It's important but not always easy to be obedient to messages that seem to come from God as a result of being quiet in prayer. It's hard to put our own wills aside and be led.[1]

LENTEN SEASON

As I reflect on my life experiences there have been many times of
turmoil and despair, but always a resolution. This is the basis of my
faith and trust that "God is our refuge and strength, a very present
help in trouble." My illness, with all of its complications and the
ultimate renewal of my body to its very healthy present condition,
really parallels the Lenten experience . . . from "Why hast thou
forsaken me?" to praise and joy and gratitude for a new beginning, a
personal resurrection.[2]

CHRISTMAS

While I have noticed for many years that God intervened in life
events, this experience has made me focus on just how often—even
constantly—that can be observed if I am open and paying attention.
. . .

The joy and celebrations of life are reflections of God's love for
us and gift to us in Jesus Christ. It's easy to be side-tracked by the
mundane, but Joseph and Mary had to go to be enrolled rather than
having their baby in a secure setting. And look at the result! We
have to remind ourselves to embrace the routine and distasteful and
look for the miracles—follow the star if you will.[3]

EASTER

I learned that there are always miracles happening and hopefully I
will be better able to recognize them. Easter is a time of renewed
hope and great new beginnings. It strengthens my faith. . . .

God is always with us and his spirit will be with us always if we allow it and seek it. . . .

Easter is a gift of forgiveness through which we all can rejoice. I like to look for Easter in many different places, even in a botanical center after a gloomy winter. . . .

The "end" for us as followers of Christ is not death but is life with the Trinity and salvation, hope, and resurrection. Our lives are different because of Easter faith.[4]

EASTERTIDE

There is an exhilaration connected with Easter that surpasses even the joy and excitement of Christmas. We are all doubting Thomases from time to time. When we despair, when things don't go as we had planned, we tend not to believe what we know to be true—just as the disciples questioned if it was really Jesus among them. Jesus's forgiveness and his demand to go and spread the word jumps out of the texts. . . .

Easter is a time of being elevated by God being in our lives from those "down" times. God intervenes through friends, associates, and even strangers who may help us move from death to finding ourselves, so that we might move forward into life.[5]

Notes

Preface

1. James F. Cobble Jr. and Charles M. Elliott, eds., *The Hidden Spirit: Discovering the Spirituality of Institutions* (Matthews, NC: Christian Ministry Resources/Christianity Today International, 1999), 34–43.

Introduction

1. James F. Hopewell, *Congregation: Stories and Structures* (Philadelphia: Fortress Press, 1987).
2. Marva Dawn and Eugene Peterson, *The Unnecessary Pastor: Rediscovering the Call* (Grand Rapids: William B. Eerdmans, 2000), 145.

Chapter 1: The Eternal Rhythm in Spiritual Practice

1. Carol Powell, "An Oasis with the Lord," *Contemplative Outreach News* 23, no. 2 (June 2008). Used by permission of the publisher.
2. Pope Benedict XVI, "Address of His Holiness Benedict XVI to the Participants in the International Congress Organized to Commemorate the 40th Anniversary of the Dogmatic Constitution on Divine Revelation 'Dei Verbum,'" September 16, 2005, http://www.vatican.va/holy_father/

benedict_xvi/speeches/2005/September/documents/hf_ ben-xvi_spe_20050916_40-dei-verbum_en.html (accessed April 16, 2009).

3. Marjorie J. Thompson, *Soul Feast: An Invitation to the Christian Spiritual Life* (Louisville, KY: Westminster/John Knox Press, 1995), 77. Used by permission of Westminster/ John Knox Press.

4. *Merriam-Webster's Collegiate Dictionary,* 11th ed., s.v. "Odyssey."

5. My book *The Base Church* (Atlanta: Forum House, 1973) was written at the beginning of the project, and my second book, *Cultivating Religious Growth Groups* (Philadelphia: Westminster Press, 1983) published the learnings of the project and applied them to congregational development.

6. Dietrich Bonhoeffer, *Life Together* (New York: Harper and Row, 1954).

Chapter 2: The Rhythm of Spiritual Formation in Time

1. Walter Wink, *The Bible in Human Transformation* (Philadelphia: Fortress Press, 1973).

2. Stanzas 1 and 3. Excerpt from *Day Is Done*, by James Quinn, S.J., Copyright (c) 1969. Reprinted by permission of the Continuum International Publishing Group. Used by permission of the publisher.

3. The Psalter, 1912, Day's Psalter, 1562.

4. "As Morning Dawns," stanzas 1 and 2. Text: Copyright (c) Fred R. Anderson; from *Singing Psalms of Joy and Praise* (Louisville: Westminster John Knox, 1986), 14. Used by permission of the copyright holder.

5. Anna Terman-White, "2008 Nebraska Five Day Academy Worship Description," March 2008, Upper Room Ministries. Used by permission of the author.

6. W. Paul Jones, "Joy and Religious Motivation," *Weavings*, November/December 1993, 38–44. Used by permission of the publisher.

7. Linda J. Vogel and Dwight W. Vogel, *Syncopated Grace: Times and Seasons with God* (Nashville: Upper Room Books, 2002), 164–65. Used by permission of the publisher.

8. James A. Thompson, "Sharing Your Story, Exploring Your Faith: A Small Group Experience Using the Church Seasons" (DMin diss., Sioux Falls Seminary, 1995), 156. Used by permission of the estate.

Chapter 3: The Waltz of the Gospel

1. Augustine, *Confessions*, trans. Francis Joseph Sheed, 2nd ed. (Cambridge, MA: Hackett, 2007), 3.

2. James P. Wind, *Inside Information*, Fall 1998: 1. Used by permission of the Alban Institute.

3. Ken Blanchard and Phil Hodges, *The Servant Leader: Transforming Your Heart, Head, Hands, and Habits* (Nashville: Thomas Nelson, 2003), 10.

4. William P. Young, *The Shack* (Los Angeles: Windblown Media, 2007).

5. Michael T. McKibben, *Orthodox Christian Meetings* (Columbus, OH: St. Ignatius of Antioch Press, 1990).

6. Dawn and Peterson, *Unnecessary Pastor*, 146. Used by permission of Wm. B. Eerdmans Publishing Co.

Chapter 4: The Christmas Triad in Churches Named Trinity

1. *To Love Is to Remember* (Overland Park, KS: Holy Trinity Orthodox Church, 2007), 5. Used by permission.

2. Ibid.

3. Ibid., 12.

4. Ibid., 17.
5. The story of Trinity Lutheran Church (LCMS) of Mission, Kansas. Used by permission.
6. Lee Hovel (senior pastor, Trinity Lutheran Church, Mission, Kansas), interview by author, January 2009.

Chapter 5: The Easter Triad in Churches Named Trinity

1. Reprinted from *Ending with Hope: A Resource for Closing Congregations* by Beth Ann Gaede, ed., with permission from the Alban Institute. Copyright © 2002 by The Alban Institute, Inc. Herndon, VA. All rights reserved. Pages 5–6.
2. Ibid., 10.
3. Ibid., 6–7.
4. Ibid., 10–11.
5. Ibid., 12–13.
6. Ibid., 14.
7. Ibid., 7.
8. Ibid., 7–8.
9. Ibid., 14.
10. The story of Trinity Lutheran Church, Omaha, Nebraska, is used by permission.
11. Natural Church Development (www.ncd-international. org) is based in Emmelsbuell, Germany. Its partner in the United States is Church Smart Resources, 3830 Ohio Ave, Saint Charles, IL 60174, www.ChurchSmart.com.
12. Trinity Lutheran Church, Omaha, Nebraska, www.trinityomaha.org.
13. Natural Church Development, *The Trinitarian Compass*, "Striving for Spiritual Balance: Why Is the Trinitarian Approach So Central for NCD?"; http://www.ncd-international.org/public/FAQ-Trinitarian.html.

Chapter 6: The Pentecost Triad in Churches Named Trinity

1. The story of Trinity Church, Omaha, Nebraska, is used by permission.
2. Trinity Church, Omaha, Nebraska, www.trinityomaha.com (accessed January 2009).
3. The story of Trinity Episcopal Church, Independence, Missouri, is used by permission.
4. Trinity Episcopal Church, Independence, Missouri, www.trinityindependence.org (accessed February 2009).

Chapter 7: Toward a New Story

1. Henry Lederle, "Treasures New and Old: Servant Leadership and the Trinity" (chapel sermon, Sterling College, Sterling, KS, May 7, 2004). Used by permission.
2. John Polkinghorne, *Quantum Physics and Theology: An Unexpected Kinship* (New Haven, CT: Yale University Press, 2007), 99–104.
3. *A Brief Statement of Faith* (Louisville, KY: Office of the General Assembly, Presbyterian Church [U.S.A.], 1990).

Chapter 8: When the Story Becomes a Song

1. James P. Wind, "Constructing Your Congregation's Story," Congregational Resource Guide, Alban Institute, http://www.congregationalresources.org/ShowOne.asp?RID=9888&TC=187 (accessed December 1, 2008). Used by permission of the Alban Institute.
2. Peter Morgan, *Story Weaving: Using Stories to Transform Your Congregation* (St. Louis: CBI Press, 1986), 50–64.
3. Charles M. Olsen, *Transforming Church Boards into Communities of Spiritual Leaders* (Herndon, VA: Alban Institute, 1995).

4. Danny E. Morris and Charles M. Olsen, *Discerning God's Will Together: A Spiritual Practice for the Church* (Nashville: Upper Room; Herndon, VA: Alban Institute, 1997).

5. Robert J. Schreiter, *Constructing Local Theologies* (Maryknoll, NY: Orbis Books, 1993), 29. Used by permission of the publisher.

6. Worshipful-Work logo. Used by permission from Water in the Desert Ministries, P.O. Box 65818, Albuquerque, NM 87193, which has been granted property rights upon the closing of Worshipful-Work.

Appendix B

1. Thompson, "Sharing Your Story, Exploring Your Faith," 158. Used by permission.

2. Ibid., 167.

3. Ibid., 162.

4. Ibid., 171–73

5. Ibid., 171, 173.

For Further Reference

Cobble, James F. Jr., and Elliott, Charles M., eds. *The Hidden Spirit: Discovering the Spirituality of Institutions.* Matthews, NC: Christian Ministry Resources/Christianity Today International, 1999.
    This book includes the contributions of a number of authors. I wrote one chapter, "Trinitarian Spirituality and Decision Making: A Structure for Congregational Stories."

Gaede, Beth Ann, ed. *Ending with Hope: A Resource for Closing Congregations.* Herndon, VA: Alban Institute, 2002.
    The specific stories of congregations that faced closing are detailed, including a Roman Catholic parish in Montana that is referenced in chapter 5 of this book. *Ending with Hope* points to resurrection; therefore, it is an Easter testimony.

Gallagher, Nora. *Things Seen and Unseen: A Year Lived in Faith.* New York: Vintage Books, 1998.
    Gallagher records church life and spiritual life in her personal reflections on the church year while engaged in yet another Trinity Church—Trinity Episcopal Church, Santa Barbara, California.

Hopewell, James F. *Congregations: Stories and Structures.* Philadelphia: Fortress Press, 1987.
    The late Dr. Hopewell opened the eyes of church leaders to the world of congregational studies with this classic intro-

duction of the role and place of story types for congregational identity.

Morgan, Peter. *Story Weaving: Using Stories to Transform Your Congregation*. St. Louis: CBI Press, 1986.
The president emeritus of the Disciples of Christ Historical Society in Nashville brings a love for congregational life and wise insight into how to tell the story and reflect on it in meaningful ways.

Olsen, Charles M. *Transforming Church Boards into Communities of Spiritual Leaders*. Herndon, VA: Alban Institute, 1995.
The four practices on which the ministry of Worshipful-Work was based are presented in one of Alban's best sellers. This current book, *The Wisdom of the Seasons*, elaborates on two of the practices—storytelling and theological reflection.

Polkinghorne, John. *Quantum Physics and Theology*. New Haven, CT: Yale University Press, 2007.
A worldwide acclaimed theologian and physicist offers intriguing insights about a trinitarian structure for the universe.

Schreiter, Robert J. *Constructing Local Theologies*. Maryknoll, NY: Orbis Books, 1993.
A member of the Society of the Precious Blood writes from his experience of listening to the culture in South America.

Thompson, James A. "Sharing Your Story, Exploring Your Faith: A Small Group Experience Using the Church Seasons." DMin diss., Sioux Falls Seminary, 1995.
The late James Thompson's unpublished Doctor of Ministry work drew from the experience of three small groups that examined their own life experiences through the wisdom of Advent, Christmas, Lent, and Easter.

Vogel, Linda J., and Dwight W. Vogel. *Syncopated Grace: Times and Seasons with God.* Nashville: Upper Room Books, 2002.

    In relating personal stories to the seasons of the church year, the Vogels sharpen our awareness of God's presence in the ordinary rhythms of life.

Wind, James P. "Constructing Your Congregation's Story," Congregational Resource Guide, Alban Institute, http://www.congregationalresources.org/ShowOne.asp?RID=9888&TC=187 (accessed December 1, 2008).

    An online adaptation of James P. Wind's *Constructing Your Congregation's Story,* which was written for the Evangelical Lutheran Church in America and published by Augsburg Fortress (1993), this helpful and timeless tool is useful for a wide range of congregations.